Unconditional Love – Unselfishness – Forgiveness –
Prayer – Persistence

Are the Only Paths that Lead to

True Success – True Happiness
Understanding of Man's and God's True Nature

And Ultimately to

GOD

Paolo Ficara
February 16, 2009
Joshua Tree, CA

This

Journey of a Healer

Volume 1

is presented to

_____

By _____

This ____ *Day*

of _____ 20__

City _____, *State* ___

Journey of a Healer, Vol. I

REVIEWS and TESTIMONIALS

Dr. Robert Harmon, M.D.
Palm Desert, California

Approximately twenty nine years ago, Paolo and I became friends. On occasion, he would recount to me his experiences in healing through prayer which he referred to as "concentration." These healings defied conventional medical belief. I, however, believed them without any doubt or hesitation as amazing as some of them were. Reading his books has been a joy and profound learning experience to me. Paolo's journey has a message for every reader.

Gessie Palazzi,
Montreal, Canada

What can I say about your manuscript? I thoroughly enjoyed it! I couldn't put it down. I am fascinated with your story (your life)! It has led me to understand many things which I didn't before. Thank you for this. And thank you for sharing your story with me.
VOLERE SIGNIFICA POTERE! " *(To want, means to be able to!)*
This is so true in life. It is a rule that everyone should apply in their lives.

Brian & Michelle Faulkner
Cherry Valley, California

The life story of Paolo Ficara is an uplifting memoir of a life well served and the amazing story about the power of prayer and the ability to heal the ill. This book will make you laugh, cry and look at life in a whole new light. A must-read for anyone interested in alternative therapy!

Ken & Elaine Osborne
Joshua Tree, California

The quest for knowledge and unimaginable love of family gives author Paolo Ficara the strength to persevere through life's conflicts and confusion. Questions that we ask deep within ourselves are a constant conflict in his life.
Is there a God?
Where is He?
Why doesn't He handle things the way we think He should?
Is there a bigger picture?
You will tread through each day with the author, feeling his fear, disappointments, excitement, financial security and most important, true love.
An inspiring and life-changing read!

Joe Salvo
Montreal, Canada

Prior to 1981, for several years, I suffered from back pain. One Sunday afternoon during the summer of that year, Paolo called me from California where he was living and asked me if I believed in God and if I believed that God could help me get well. I answered yes. At my reply, he suggested I visit the Saint Joseph Oratory and pray to God, Saint Joseph and Brother Andrew with sincerity and humility. He was going also to pray for me from his house. I did as suggested. Three days later, my pain went away and I have been fine since.

Giuseppe Sutera Sardo
Montreal, Canada

Journey of a Healer is the marvelous journey of Paolo Ficara. From the very first pages, you enter into a different world. Adventures, mysticism, religions, meditation, healings, belief in a supernatural world and understanding are the things that make this book and his life story unique.

Anybody belonging to any type of religion could read this book, because there is no particular religion preferred but one entity that could be anyone's. I consider myself very lucky because I had the chance to read the complete story when I needed it most. It helped me to change and improve my life and the one of my family.

I hope that after publishing the first volume the author will publish the other two volumes immediately, because I believe they can do a lot of good for a lot of people.

Lori Nelson
Erie, Pennsylvania

I met Paolo (Paul) Ficara and his wife Pina in 2003. I just graduated from Business College. I was applying for jobs that I wasn't sure that I was even qualified for. I was feeling good about myself because I was 35 years old when I went back to school and never thought in a million years I would be successful. I proved myself wrong and actually loved being in school. Now, once again I was back to feeling vulnerable about where I fit in the working world.

When I met Paolo (Paul), he was like nobody that I ever had the pleasure to encounter in my whole life. I felt so welcome in his home and we hit it off immediately. I was very interested in what he had to say. He told me that he was a spiritual person and helped people to achieve their goals. He was also a healing man. People went to him for many personal reasons.

He asked me what my goals were in life, where I wanted to be as a person. I told him about the job that I applied for at a local hospital in my community. He said that I needed to focus on wanting the job and to pray and ask for what I wanted. I always thought that it was selfish to ask for something for yourself. But I did what he told me and darn if I didn't get that job! For the first time in my life I took a different approach at going after what I wanted. This was new to me. I felt on top of the world.

I have been focused on my life and concentrate on where my life is going. Do I feel it is going in the direction that I want it? Yes, I am in control now and it feels great. I pray for what I want and am grateful everyday for the gifts that I receive. Thanks to Paolo (Paul), he has shown me the good side of life and even myself. I like the person that I've become. I do believe "If you ask you shall receive." I don't feel selfish as long as I'm asking for help to became a better me.

I may have only met Paolo (Paul) once for a brief moment, in my life, but I will never forget him and his words stay with me always. I think of him and his wife often. He was definitely a positive impact in my life and the best way that I can thank him is to be the best that I can be. I wish him and his family all the happiness life has to offer and I hope that one day I can talk with him again.

Debbie Williams
July 7, 1981, Cathedral City, California

On June 23, 1981 I was recovering from a knee operation. I had a childhood injury where they had to completely remove my right knee cap. The bone was deteriorating from the injury and it had to be scraped.

It was extremely painful and I was limping. I could not bend it at all or put any pressure on it what so ever.

Paolo (Paul) Ficara had discussed my leg operation and disability with me. He asked if he could help me. He said that through his healing ability and God's help, he thought he could help me to heal and walk.

I went over to Paolo's house and he told me to completely relax in a chair and to pray and concentrate that my leg would get better. (This would happen only if I believed in God.)

I relaxed and as Paolo helped me, I could feel my leg completely relax. I became so relaxed that I fell into a semi-sleep. I would hear some background noises, but it was as if I was in a deep sleep.

As we prayed and concentrated on my leg, it became warmer and warmer.

When I woke up, I was completely refreshed. I got up and found I could walk with no limp.

It also did not hurt anymore as it had. The leg felt warm on the inside but still cold in the outside.

The next morning my leg felt great.

It has been 2 weeks and it still does not hurt as it did and it is not stiff.

The only discomfort is a little stiffness from not moving it for so long, (2.5 to 3 months).

I went to my physician today and he told me since I had seen him last that I has made remarkable improvement and I was completely released from my doctors care. The Doctor helped my leg but I truly feel that it was Paolo that healed it.

Thank you.

JOURNEY OF A HEALER

Volume I

The Struggle

By

PAOLO FICARA

JOURNEY OF A HEALER
VOLUME I *The Struggle*

Copyright © 2009 Paolo Ficara.
All rights reserved. This book may not be reproduced in any form without the consent of the author.

Printed in the United States of America. No part of this book may be used or reproduced in any manner whatsoever without written permission except in the case of brief quotations embodied in critical articles or reviews.

For information contact:

Minoa Publishing, LLC
P.O. Box #370
Yucca Valley, CA 92286

ISBN: 978-0-615-26775-3

Typography and Cover: Kirk Thomas, www.kirks-graphics.com

DEDICATION

*I dedicate this work of mine to the memory of my
beloved parents, Pellegrino (Pino) and Rosa Ficara ...*

*... for having instilled in my mind and my heart
the basic principles of honesty, love
and respect for mankind.*

*Grazie di Cuore Papa
Grazie di Cuore Mamma
Your loving son,
Paolo*

THE AUTHOR

Since my childhood in Sicily, I have searched for the key to understanding this life on earth. I have questioned God's existence and what seems to be His mysterious and at times senseless and contradictory behavior.

At the age of fourteen, I witnessed the miraculous healing of my terminally ill mother. This experience profoundly affected my life, instilling in me the desire to learn how healing occurs and who God is in His true essence and nature.

Born to a poor family of farmers, my older brother hoped to help the family financially by emigrating to Germany at the young age of eighteen.

This caused my brother, myself and my entire family a lot of pain. It was during this period that I promised myself to reunite my family in a place where we could live, work and prosper together.

In the hopes of fulfilling this promise, I emigrated to Montreal, Canada in September of 1967 at the age of twenty-one. There I met my wife Pina with whom I had three children.

In August 1979, I moved my family to Joshua Tree, a small town in the southern California desert. Here, in the peace and harmony of this new and different environment, I learned how to pray, how to forgive and most importantly, how to love. As a result, I was finally able to fulfill all my dreams—including my quest to find the answers to the questions I'd been asking myself and others for most of my life.

I discovered that the limitations man puts on himself and the problems man encounters—including those of health, finances, love and discontent—are solely the fruits of ignorance. I strongly believe that anyone can attain success, good health and happiness.

Now nearing retirement as owner of a small asphalt paving company, I am working on my next book, a comparison of modern religions, and look forward to spending more time nurturing the Universal Center for Self-Enlightenment and Self-Healing—a foundation I have established to help others find success and fulfillment.

I humbly pray that my life story can inspire and help each reader to find his own journey through this life and that he would experience a brighter and more successful future.

I thank all those who, after reading my words, will take the time to share their learning's with as many people as they can. I believe that in so doing, not only they will be more fulfilled, but they also will contribute to improve other people's lives, making this world a better place to live.

Finally, I hope that everyone's desires will be fulfilled and that the peace, the harmony and the joy of God will abide with them today, tomorrow and forever.

God bless,

Paolo Ficara
February -16 - 2009

Journey of a Healer, Vol. I

ACKNOWLEDGEMENTS

I would like to thank the people who have influenced the course of my life. I will start with my family.

I thank my wife Pina, my three children, Pellegrino (Pino), Antonino (Nino) and Paolo Jr., my parents Pellegrino (Pino) and Rosa Ficara, and my brothers Gioacchino and Ignazio for their deep, unconditional and unselfish love that always showed. I also thank them for always believing in me; for being there when I needed them most; for giving me support and hope in my darkest and most difficult moments; and for the joy they continuously give me. It is impossible to express in words the magnitude of my appreciation and devotion for what they have done for me.

The only regret I have with regards to our relationship is my incapacity to shower them with words the immensity of my love and the infinite gratitude I always felt for all of them. For that I ask their forgiveness.

I thank Zia (aunt) Carmela, my mother's only sister, and her husband Zio (uncle) Salvatore Piazza, for having sponsored my parents and my brother Ignazio, helping them to settle in their new land, and for their love for all of us. They have been instrumental in making our dreams become reality. Without their help, the course of our lives would have been completely different.

I thank Zio Joe Piazza, Zio Agostino Piazza and Zio Luca Piazza, Zio Salvatore's brothers, and their family for accepting us as part of their family and making us feel welcome and at home.

I thank Zio Lillo, my father's younger brother, and Zia Lina, his wife, for being like second parents to me; and their two sons

Gioacchino and Antonio for always treating me like a brother.

I thank Zio Pasquale Salvo and his wife, Zia Antonina, their children Pietro and his wife Nena, Joe and his wife Angie, Giovanni and his wife Angela, Mattia and her husband Zio Nino Gentile, and Antonietta and her husband Nino Caci, for accepting me as one of their family and for always being there for us.

I thank my cousin Francesca and her husband Giovanni Sciangula, my cousin Maria and her husband Pasquale Terrasi, and my cousin Teresa and her husband Carmelo Tortorici, and my friends Liborio Zambito, Vincenzo D'Anna and Emanuele Territo for helping me overcome the difficult times I went through during my first few months in Montreal.

Other people who have influenced the course of my life are some of my closest friends. I would like to give thanks to Enzo Tortorici, Giuseppe Zabbara, Pippo Sutera, Franco Sferra, Giuseppe Cortese and Pippo Ferrera for their brotherly friendship.

A special thanks goes to:
- My friend Joe Catalano, for having treated me as a brother from the very first moment we met in Palm Springs, and for helping me to establish my paving company when first I arrived in Southern California.
- My friend Edoardo Federico, for helping me to settle in Joshua Tree when we moved to California..
- My friend, Professor Eliseo Franco Amico, PhD, for putting all his heart, passion, love and talent in translating my manuscript from its original Italian format into English, and for having over the course of the years challenged my experiences and my thoughts. He has been more a brother than a friend.
- My friend Robert Harmon, M.D., for believing in my healing stories and for tirelessly encouraging me to pursue my life's natural vocation.
- My friend Dr. Beverly Marie Rumsey. Thanks to her highly

developed sense of clairvoyance, she helped our family avoid what could have been a very unpleasant experience.
- Thanks to my editors, Roberta Edgar and Sandy Tritt, for helping me to edit the manuscript.
- Thanks to Kirk Thomas, for his help in assisting me in the publication of the manuscript.

I would like to thank all my relatives, friends, and acquaintances who directly or indirectly, in a positive or negative way, influenced and shaped the course of my life. I forgive and thank all the people who directly or indirectly have caused me grief and pain, because I know, without those experiences, I could not have become the person I am today. To everyone I give my eternal appreciation, gratitude and love.

- I acknowledge and thank Thomas Nelson Bibles, a Division of Thomas Nelson, Inc., for allowing me to include verses from the *The Holy Bible, New King James Version*, Copyright 1992, by Thomas Nelson, Inc.
- I acknowledge and thank Wikipedia, the Free Encyclopedia from the Internet, for allowing me to include reports and notations about characters.

I would also like to thank the following people who through their works and their writings have immensely influenced the outcome of my life:

- Joseph Murphy, author of *The Power of Your Subconscious Mind*, for teaching me the importance of our thoughts.
- Baird T. Spalding, author of *Masters of the Far East*, for explaining the endless capability of Man.
- Paramhansa Yogananda, author of *Autobiography of a Yogi* and founder of Self Realization Fellowship, for teaching me how to pray and meditate.

A special acknowledgement and thanks go to:
- Lord Jesus
- Lord Buddha

- Lord Krishna
- Prophet Mohammed
- Prophet Moses

I thank Them for teaching me that the path that deliver us from the bondage of ignorance, limitation, poverty, misery, and sufferance, and that will lead us to experience success, riches, freedom, and Divine Joy, is one and the same and can only be achieved through prayer, love and forgiveness.

I was astonished to learn that the essence of their teachings, messages, ideals and ideas, although expressed in different words and different ways, are expressing the same truth; which when interpreted and accepted correctly and lived faithfully, will lead and take us to the same destination, to the source where we all come from, to God, so we can learn to understand Him, so we can learn to know Him, and so finally, we can be reunited to His essence for eternity.

Finally, I give my thanks to the Creative Power (God), that abides within me, that abides within every living man and women, that abides in every living creature, and that abides in every atom existing in the universe, for having:

- Inspired me every moment of my life;
- Guided me in every step of my life;
- Paved the right path for me to follow;
- Assisted me in all my pursuits;
- Fulfilled all my dreams, desires, aspirations, goals and prayers;
- And most importantly, for having unfolded to me the apparent mystery of life, allowing me to perceive what is the true essence and nature of man, what is the true essence and nature of God, and what is the relationship existing between them.

Once more, to all of them go my love, my devotion and my gratitude.

Paolo Ficara

Journey of a Healer, Vol. I

North America Journey

Paolo Ficara

European Journey

CONTENTS

INTRODUCTION XXI
1 Childhood. 1
2 Early Questions. 12
3 Early School Years 17
4 Mother's Miraculous Healing 21
5 Return to School. 27
6 New School. 37
7 First Love 41
8 First Trip to Germany 48
9 Trip to Ribera 53
10 Graduation – Lessons from My Parents. 59
11 In Love Again and Future Plans. 68
12 Travels, Military Service and Engagement 79
13 Montreal. 86
14 From Joy to Disillusionment 93
15 Dark and Challenging Days 104
16 I Meet the Girl of My Dreams … 111
17 First Job, Engagement, First Business 126
18 Marriage. 136
19 Father's Illness 149
20 Calgary and Waterbury 157
21 First Child, First Home 166
22 Father's Death and Business Disaster 174
23 First Encounter with a Clairvoyant 183
24 James Bay 195
25 Encounter with a Healer 205
26 Second Child, First Healing 219
27 Our Own Company 229

Paolo Ficara

INTRODUCTION

Journey of a Healer is the story of my life: a Sicilian farm boy who grew up in a financially poor environment surrounded by the deep love of my family.

In this first of three volumes, I recall my childhood in beautiful native Ribera, my immigration to North America, and my struggles during the first ten years of my life in this new land. Born to a Catholic family, my parents raised me to fear and love God. For that reason, for my kindergarten and first three years of elementary school, I was sent to a small institute operated by Catholic nuns. There, I not only learned the basics of how to read and write, but I also I learned the basics about God and Jesus.

I was taught that God is the creator of the universe, that He is everywhere, that He knows everything, that He loves us very much, that we need to pray to Him all the time, and that He is the giver of everything we have. I was also taught the story of Adam and Eve, the story of the life, works, and teachings of Jesus, and the mystery of God's Trinity.

When I was fourteen, my mother became deathly ill. The doctors could do nothing for her. As a last resort, my family took her to a healer, and I assisted with her miraculous healing. The experience was overwhelming.

When I asked the healer how she had healed my mother, she answered that her ability to heal people was a special gift received from God. Although I was young, I didn't accept her explanation. If God existed and if He were as good and caring as everybody thought, how could He show preference for certain people?

Not being able to come up with an acceptable explanation for my mother's healing, I was bewildered. After days of deep thinking, incapable of understanding what had happened, I promised myself I would do whatever it took to discover the truth.

I wanted to know:
- **How did such healings take place?**
- **How and why did miracles happen?**
- **Why were few people healed in miraculous ways?**
- **Why did so few have this incredible power to heal?**
- **Who, in His true essence, is this God, that throughout time people from all over the world have spoken of Him, yet there is no tangible evidence that anyone has seen Him face-to-face or spoken with Him?**
- **Is God for real, or is He just an imagining of the human mind?**

At age eighteen, my older brother immigrated to Germany, where he worked as a construction laborer and sent money for me to go to school. His departure left great grief on the hearts of each member of our family. While I was still in school, I promised myself to do whatever it took to one day reunite my family in a place where we could all live, work and prosper together. For that reason, after I graduated, I immigrated first to Germany, then to Canada, and ultimately to the U.S.A.

During the winter of 1974-75, while living in Montreal, I was strangely led to a bookstore, where the clerk suggested I purchase "The Power of Your Subconscious Mind" by Joseph Murphy.

This was the turning point of my life.

The author affirmed that man is endowed with two levels of mind—the Conscious and the Subconscious. The Conscious Mind allows him to think and to create thoughts, while the Subconscious Mind, which is the seat of man's Creative Power, manifests in man's life whatever he conceives with his Conscious Mind in the form of thoughts—so the experiences of our life, good or bad, are the consequence of what we think and believe.

Could this be true?

Could our thoughts really be responsible for all our experiences?

While debating this, I recalled my mother's miraculous healing.

Who healed my mother? God, who empowered the healer, as she suggested, or the power of our thoughts in the form of prayer?

My thirst to answer this question motivated me to search for answers. Over a lifetime, I have discovered some answers that I will share within the pages of these volumes. To better understand the message of this book, I suggest reading all three volumes chronologically and slowly. In time, you will understand the reason for my suggestion.

To everyone, my blessing and my most sincere wish of good luck.

Paolo Ficara

Via Gerone #53 Ribera, Agrigento, Sicily, Italy

The front of the house was on this street lined with balconies.

CHAPTER 1
Childhood

I was born Paolo Ficara in February 1946, in Ribera, Province of Agrigento, a town of approximately 20,000 located in southern Sicily, about four miles off the Mediterranean coast. The town, according to a local historian by the name of Raimondo Lentini, dates back to 1635. A group of people from the neighboring town of Caltabellotta working the flourishing rice fields, tired of traveling back and forth, decided to build their houses closer to where they were working. They chose the plain of San Nicola, today known as the Quartiere (neighborhood) of Sant' Antonino, giving origin to their own community.

I was born and raised in this *quartiere*, more precisely in via Gerone # 53. The name *Ribera* was given by the Prince of Paterno' Don Luigi Moncada, who ruled the area at the time, in honor of his beautiful wife Maria Afan de Ribera, daughter of the Duca di Alcala'.

From an historic perspective, Ribera is relatively young for Sicily, where some municipalities go back thousands of years.

The terrain in and around Ribera is mostly hilly, dotted here and there with small plains. The town is crossed by three small rivers, the Verdura, the Magazzolo and the Platani, which provide vital irrigation for local agriculture. Whereas the previous efforts of local farmers were almost exclusively limited to the cultivation of cereals, technological developments of the late 1960s made it possible for Ribera's highly versatile and creative inhabitants to produce an abundance of vineyards, fruit orchards, and citrus groves, the fruits of which are

Gioacchino & Carmela Ficara – my father's parents

Antonina & Paolo Tortorici – my mother's parents

Chapter 1

exported throughout Italy and much of Europe. The socioeconomic boost to the region has been substantial.

Ribera's rainy season extends through autumn, winter, and spring, making the dry, mild summers ideal for tourism. I recall summer nights spent under glittering stars or limpid moonlight with my father Pino, my brother Gioacchino, and my grandfather Paolo—an excellent storyteller who delighted us with yarns of "the good old days" when he was younger, as was Ribera.

My father was born into a family of sixteen children, of which only four daughters and three sons survived. The others were lost to malaria, a common cause of infant mortality in those days. Fifth among the surviving children and the second male, Pellegrino "Pino" Ficara was a tall, vigorous man endowed with a strong personality and highly regarded for his honesty and levelheadedness. His life revolved around his family, whom he loved and cherished above all else. The primary focus of his existence was to make possible for his children all those things he had been deprived of as a youth.

Although austere in appearance, he was kind and sensitive, constantly showering his family with love and affection which, although not expressed in words, came straight from his heart. By his example and good manners, he taught his children to be kind, respectful, and honest. However, he would not hesitate to use stern measures to get his point across whenever he thought it necessary. My father never attended school, so he could not read or write. This handicap was a genuine tragedy for him, and he never failed to remind us of the difficulties facing those with no formal training. As he saw it, education allowed individuals to tackle life's problems with greater ease, and for that reason, he encouraged us to enjoy learning and excel in our classes. His greatest dream was to see us the proud recipients of a high school diploma or, better yet, a university degree.

Around 1906 at age twenty, my maternal grandfather, Paolo—like so many other Italians—immigrated to America hoping to find a better future. He settled in the New York City borough of the Bronx, where he met and married my grandmother, Antonina. Before long the couple moved to Waterbury, Connecticut, to be closer to Grandfather Paolo's older brother Giuseppe. There he worked as a laborer for the city, setting aside as much income as possible to purchase property in Ribera for his retirement years.

Because many U.S. banks were going bankrupt at that time, all my grandparents' savings were sent to his parents in Ribera for safekeeping. In 1913, their first child, Carmela, was born.

By 1920, following the first world war, my grandparents had saved enough money to buy a beautiful house and sufficient farm land to secure their financial future, so they moved back to Ribera as planned.

When they arrived in Ribera, they discovered their savings had been spent on dowries for the other children. This left my grandparents with an unpleasant choice: return to the United States in shame or remain in Ribera. They chose to stay in Ribera.

Incurring huge debt in the process, they bought a small house and some land on credit.

My mother, Rosa, was born in Ribera in July, 1923. She was the second and last child in the family. Meanwhile, Carmela, accustomed to the comfort and affluence of life in America, could not adjust to the relative poverty of Ribera. In 1926, at age thirteen, she asked for and was granted permission to return to America. Her parents hoped to rejoin her after getting their finances in order, but their plans were never realized. My grandfather did not live to see her again.

Upon her return to the United States, Carmela went to live with her aunt—a sister of my grandmother Antonina—in Elizabeth, New Jersey. A few years later, Carmela moved to Waterbury, Connecticut, where she married and spent the rest of her life.

Since my grandparents lacked the funds to buy my mother the required textbooks, she was forced to drop out of school after first grade. She was sent to a woman who taught her to embroider and crochet, a craft she enjoys even now at 83. In accordance with the

Chapter 1

*Various pictures of Piazza Corso Umberto I,
Ribera, Agrigento birth town of the author.*

Another view of Piazza Corso Umberto I, Ribera, Agrigento

Easter Sunday in Ribera - 1995

Chapter 1

The family farm house where in my youth I spent most of my summers.

custom of the day, her parents betrothed her to my father at age 18, and they were married on April 18, 1942. Six months later, after Mussolini committed the country to a wartime alliance with Germany, my father was inducted into the Italian army, leaving my mother pregnant and in the care of my maternal grandparents.

In February, 1943, my mother gave birth to a beautiful child, whom she named Gioacchino after my paternal grandfather.

The family's wartime experience was characterized by terror and deprivation. Fearing Allied air bombardments, my grandparents, mother, and brother moved out into the country where they felt safer, but where they were deprived of even the most basic of necessities. Eventually, the United States led the Allied forces to victory over Hitler's armies, bringing the war to an end. In the spring of 1945, my father, still physically fit, was able to return to his life in Ribera.

Soon after, my mother became pregnant again, and in February 1946, I was brought into the world and named for my maternal

Gioacchino Ficara at 6 years of age and Paolo Ficara at 3.

Chapter 1

Paolo at 6 with Grandfather Paolo and brother Gioacchino age 9.

grandfather Paolo. Ten years later, in April, 1956, a third boy was born into the family. Once again, my parents followed tradition and named their child for an elder family member. This time it was Ignazio, after my father's eldest brother.

A small woman, my mother is very thoughtful, sensitive and endowed with a great and deep love for her family. To this day she continues to devote her life to home and family.

As far back as I can remember, my mother suffered with health problems. The symptoms were always the same: severe headaches and vomiting spells that kept her bedridden for a few days to a few weeks. On two occasions, she was saved in ways that were nothing short of miraculous. These healing events were so momentous they redefined the purpose of my life.

Upon completion of the equivalent of junior high at the age of fifteen, my eldest brother Gioacchino began working in the fields with my father. Over the course of my life, I have learned a great deal from my brother, who has been one of the greatest examples of personal sacrifice, love, and altruism that I have ever known. It has been no less than a blessing from God to have a brother like him, for his lofty example has been a constant source of inspiration to me, contributing to a greater understanding and deeper love for my family.

Chapter 1

Paolo Ficara's Confirmation and First Communion at age 9.

CHAPTER 2
Early Questions

Given the harmonious relationship existing between my parents, I grew up in a serene family atmosphere. Having been raised in a religious environment, my mother nurtured her children with love and respect for God and made sure we attended Holy Mass every Sunday. As a result, I spent my kindergarten and my first three years of elementary school in classes run by Catholic nuns.

Those nuns revealed to us the following principles as pure gospel:
- **The universe was created by God.**
- **We are all children of God.**
- **God is a triune being, or three persons in one: the Father, the Son and the Holy Ghost.**
- **God is Omnipotent, Omnipresent, and Omniscient.**
- **God loves us very much.**

They also revealed the story of Adam and Eve, whose disobedience to God's injunction not to eat the famous forbidden fruit became the "original sin." Their ensuing expulsion from the Garden of Eden condemned to death and eternal suffering not only themselves, but all generations to follow, including everyone alive today.

God was so grieved for the sad plight of humanity and so moved by His deep love for His children, He sent His only begotten son, Jesus (none other than God Himself as a member of the Holy Trinity), to be crucified and die in order to redeem mankind from Adam's and Eve's original sin.

Chapter 2

Jesus' sacrifice, and the baptism He instituted, would save us from eternal perdition—hence the nuns persistently exhorted us to adore and love Jesus and God.

Despite the credible source of this information, when I was not out playing with other kids, I would reflect on what the nuns were teaching. I couldn't help but wonder.

- **Who is God?**
- **Who does He resemble?**
- **Where does He dwell?**
- **Why haven't I ever heard of someone who has personally seen or spoken with Him?**

Despite my young age, I wanted to understand such things as the mystery of the Holy Trinity.

- **How could God the father, Jesus the son, and the Holy Ghost be one single entity?**
- **How could God know what thoughts exist in the mind of every individual?**
- **How could He know the past, present and future of the human race?**
- **What sort of brain could He have that would allow him to remember all those things?**

Another thing that left me quite perplexed was the Adam and Eve episode.

- **If God is truly Omniscient and knows everything there is to know, why didn't He realize Adam and Eve would not resist the temptation of eating the forbidden fruit?**
- **Considering that He created Adam and Eve, why did He not give them the fortitude to withstand the serpent's temptation?**
- **Since the disobedience was essentially caused by a flaw in the character that God Himself had endowed Adam and**

Eve, why did He go into a frenzy and chase them out of the Garden of Eden, condemning them and their progeny to eternal pain, misery and despair?
- How could God condemn all of humanity for the mistakes of two people?
- Was it their fault they were not strong enough to resist Satan's lure?
- Why did He put them through such a demanding test?
- If God truly loves the human race, and is as good and compassionate as He is reputed to be, why didn't He choose to forgive them?

Despite the fact that I was a child at the time, my questions were deep and complex—and the list was endless:
- Were God's actions really fair?
- How could Jesus' death redeem us from the sins of Adam and Eve?
- How could the baptism instituted by Jesus have the power to free us from original sin?
- How could the sprinkling salt and water over our heads make possible our rebirth into a new, unblemished existence— and, according to Catholic ritual, deliver us from sin?
- If the baptism really has the power to free us of the original sin, should we not also be liberated from pain and sorrow and our lives filled with eternal bliss and joy?
- Why then do people continue to live in misery and suffering without an apparent way out?

In light of these unanswered questions, I began to seriously doubt the validity of what I was being taught in school.

One time, I asked the school priest, who taught religion, to help me understand these enigmas. He suggested I was a smart ass, and if I didn't stop asking such asinine questions, he would throw me out

Chapter 2

of class. Since my questions were heartfelt and dictated by a genuine desire to grasp what was a complete mystery to me, the priest's reply left me more perplexed than ever. I felt that if I could only understand, it would be easier to develop a deeper faith and love for God and Jesus.

In my growing curiosity and gnawing doubt, I asked the parish priest to help me understand. "You're too young to understand," he replied. At that point, I gave up my search for a rational explanation.

After completing five years of elementary school, I enrolled in a special three-year agricultural training program. Due to space limitations, the school offered two sessions: one in the morning and one in the afternoon. The morning session was "mixed" in that it was attended by both boys and girls. The session in the afternoon was strictly reserved for boys. I was admitted to the latter.

The first day of school, the professor told us of a saying by Italian poet and writer Vittorio Alfieri:

"VOLERE, SIGNIFICA POTERE!"
Which can be translated as:
"TO WANT, MEANS TO BE ABLE TO!"

He explained that our success in life mostly is conditioned by our will and determination to succeed. For that reason, he encouraged us to study very hard and in time we would see our effort and hard work pay dividends.

My first reaction to his words was negative. At that time, I believed our success in life mainly is determined by our natural capability and intelligence. Therefore, what the professor was saying could not be true.

Later on, I would discover I was completely wrong.

*Paolo center at age 16 with his two best friends,
Enzo Tortorici on left and Giuseppe Zabbara on the right.*

CHAPTER 3
Early School Years

While I was in sixth grade, I developed a close friendship with two classmates—Giuseppe Zabbara and Enzo Tortorici. As of this writing, our brotherly bond continues to flourish, even stronger than ever.

Until the seventh grade, I was never regarded as particularly bright. I passed my classes with a bare minimum C average and was inclined to think that success in school depended on natural gifts—which I assumed I lacked. Despite this attitude, I had a keen interest in what was going on in my family. During the summer or whenever school was out, I went into the fields and helped my father however I could—discovering in the tranquility of the natural landscape a degree of happiness I could experience nowhere else.

At that point in my life, it occurred to me that perhaps school was not my fated lot and that I would be much better off following in my father's footsteps as a farmer.

Beginning with the 1958 school year—my third in the agricultural training program—something occurred that, though seemingly unimportant at the time, turned out to be extremely significant, in as much as it laid the foundation that changed the course of my life.

A few days before the beginning of the school year, I passed by the school to check my schedule of classes. I discovered my friend Enzo Tortorici and I had been transferred to the morning "mixed" section.

Even though I ordinarily didn't show it, I was a shy boy, and the thought of sitting in a classroom with girls made me nervous. The thought of being called upon in class and being unable to answer the teacher's questions in front of all those girls embarrassed me. I realized I had to conquer my timidity and excel in my studies. There I was at age twelve, looking at my far-from-impressive grades from the preceding years. I feared I was not intelligent enough to be an above-average student, and I was therefore doomed to academic mediocrity. On the other hand, I refused to admit defeat, and I was able to convince myself that with some effort I could become a model student capable of competing with the top of my class.

For the first time in my life, pride spurred me to succeed in my studies. Moreover, my friend Enzo Tortorici was one of the brightest boys in school, and the idea of emulating him became a motivating factor in my drive toward higher goals.

From the first day of class, I paid greater attention to my teachers and did my homework diligently in the evenings. I noticed that tasks that had previously appeared difficult now became easier to perform. I continued my efforts in earnest, and by the end of the first school term, I had achieved higher than average grades—something I previously had never been able to do.

That experience demonstrated that my prior lack of academic success was not so much caused by lack of intelligence as it was by insufficient effort. I understood that practically everyone has the capacity to learn, but success depends mostly on the sheer willingness to do the work.

For me, that was a valuable discovery and the most important lesson in my young life. In other words, wanting something badly was the most efficient pathway toward attaining it, and it was through continuous effort that one was capable of reaching even the most sought-after dreams. I realized Alfieri's saying, ***"VOLERE SIGNIFICA POTERE!" (To Want Means To Be Able To!)*** which I heard almost two years before from my Italian professor, was an incredible reality. Over the course of my life, I had the pleasure and the joy to experience that truth many times over.

The validity of that saying came also to me soon after. Every Sunday, my mother gave my brother Gioacchino and me the equivalent of fifty

Chapter 3

cents each, and told us to spend half of it on the price of a movie ticket and the remainder on sweets from the local pastry shop. But instead of buying the sweets as my mother suggested, I acquired the habit of buying cigarettes and smoking them while watching the movie. Like the majority of boys in my age group, I emulated the older boys, thereby creating a false image of maturity.

One night, as I smoked while watching a film, I felt nausea. A headache and vomiting followed. It was apparent to me that smoking was the cause of my problem, so I went outside for some fresh air, hoping to relieve my symptoms. After about ten minutes, I felt better. Then, realizing how stupidly I had behaved, I threw my remaining cigarettes to the ground and stomped on them. Not only had I disobeyed my parents who sacrificed their hard-earned money to allow my brother and me to have fun, but I got sick on top of it all. So, I asked myself a few pertinent questions:

- **Could anyone act more moronic than I had?**
- **Why was I poisoning my body?**
- **What benefit did I derive from smoking?**
- **Was I proving to anyone, or even to myself, I had grown up?**

Despite my relatively young age, something inside of me suggested that smoking was simply a charade, an illusion whose end result was the destruction of the human body. I promised myself that I would never touch another cigarette, and I have kept my pledge.

I fully realized how bizarre human behavior can be when we try to conform to the dangerous whims of our peers. Sadly, I have noticed the same psychological aberrations exist today. Whereas in previous generations, children were primarily rooted in the abuse of tobacco, children of the current generation indulge in drugs and alcohol—creating a lethal compound with a profoundly more lethal kick. If it does nothing else, I hope my youthful smoking habit demonstrates it is never too early or too late to give up a bad habit if we effectively tap into our willpower.

The 1958 school year was one of the most marvelous periods in my life. I finished among the top students in my class and was justifiably proud of my accomplishment. Now, at least, I was aware of my capabilities. I had nothing to envy of anyone, and if I wanted, I could attain any goal I fixed my mind to.

Nevertheless, my happiness was short-lived. Soon I had to face the reality that I wouldn't be able to pursue my studies because there was no technical high school in my hometown. My parents did not have the financial resources to send me to another city. I wondered why now that I excelled in my schoolwork I was being forced to give it up. Still, instead of being disheartened, I held dear the positive experiences of that year, and I hoped that somehow a miracle would occur that would grant me the return to my beloved books.

But what miracle could change the financial condition of my family? Only one: winning the lottery. I spent my entire week's allowance on lottery tickets, hoping for a miracle. By October, the schools opened their doors for the new academic year, but I wasn't going back. The miracle had not happened. Even though from a logical perspective I knew I could not return to school, I held onto the hope and dream that someday it would happen.

CHAPTER 4
Mother's Miraculous Healing

Around that time, my father and brother advised me to stop working in the fields and begin an apprenticeship with a local mechanic named Serafino Samaritano. Approximately three months after I began working at Serafino's garage, my mother fell ill with recurrent headaches and vomiting spells. The doctors prescribed medications and assured the family she would soon get well. The days went by, but the prescription drugs had no effect. Instead of getting better, she was getting a lot worse.

Further discussions with the doctors were of no help. The doctors didn't know what was ailing her, but whatever it was, according to them, was not critical. I noticed my mother growing progressively weaker and paler, reaching the point where she could no longer get off the bed on her own. My father asked me to stop working so I could care for her at home.

Under my mother's careful and patient supervision, I learned how to cook and take care of household chores. With her drawn-out illness, the family funds diminished until there was absolutely nothing left. One day I searched the house for money for her medicine and found nothing. I was worried, and worse, I showed it.

Detecting my frame of mind, my mother called me to her bedside and asked what was bothering me.

"We're broke," I replied. "There's no money for your medicine."

"Go get my purse." She pointed at the wardrobe where she hid her purse.

After wading through a pile of clothes, I found her purse. I opened it and discovered a treasury of coins. Ecstatic, I rushed to my mother's bedside and handed her the purse. She turned her head and fixed her deep-set, feverish eyes on me. Her face reflected all the sadness in her soul, displaying that look of resigned acceptance typical of someone awaiting death.

Holding her tears in a determined effort to help me maintain control of my own emotions, she whispered, "The coins are from the sale of leftover milk from our two goats. I had intended them as a surprise—new suits for Gioacchino, Ignazio and you, Paolo." Unable to restrain her emotions any longer, she sobbed. "I will probably never get to see the day I can do that for you." Then with a complex gesture of defeat and resignation, she added, "Perhaps it is the will of God." Then, she fell back onto her pillow.

Touched by the deep love she bore for us, I told her with tears in my own eyes, "Don't worry about our suits. Concentrate on getting well. After that, God willing, we will get our new clothes."

I couldn't help thinking how lucky I was to have such a mother, and, at the same time, how unfortunate, for I could see that despite all the doctors' efforts to restore her health, she was getting inexorably worse. What hurt me the most was my inability to help her.

I prayed to God and Jesus, asking them to guide the doctors in making a proper diagnosis and finding the true cause of my mother's illness—but nothing ever happened. Even so, I kept repeating to myself that God could not allow my mother to die, as my brothers and I were so in need of her help and love.

I desperately clung to hope and sensed something was going to happen that would restore her health. For a few days, I continuously prayed to that effect.

One evening not long after, one of my mother's cousins came to visit her. After noticing she was practically immobilized, the cousin called my father aside and said she sensed that my mother's illness had not been induced by natural causes, but by an "artificial" one: sorcery.

Chapter 4

According to her theory, this was the reason the prescribed drugs had produced no healing.

She said she knew of an old woman near the city of Marsala, approximately 75 miles from our hometown, who was renowned for restoring the health of those who suffered or were victims of sorcery—and we should take my mother to her immediately.

No one in my family believed in the occult, and our expressions registered our skepticism—particularly in the case of my father. The cousin became angry when she saw our resistance and raised her voice, asserting the validity of her opinion and demanding we consider her advice.

After attempting to calm her down and expressing thanks for her advice, my father agreed to give the matter due consideration. A few moments later, he called us children aside and suggested that since the doctors were no longer giving us any hope, we had the responsibility and the duty to try whatever was suggested, regardless of whether or not we believed in it. "With the exception of the cost of the rental car, what have we to lose by going to Marsala? Isn't it worth the gamble to try to make a last effort to save your mother's life?"

That evening, my father rented a car, and we left for Marsala to meet with the old woman. Upon our arrival early the next morning, we were surprised to see such a large number of cars crowded in front of her house—and people lined up for an audience with her.

At precisely seven o'clock, a small, elderly woman opened the door and faced the crowd. In deference to my mother's frail condition, my father respectfully asked the bystanders to allow us to pass through first, which they did without exception. The urgency of the situation was obvious to all.

Since my mother could not stand, we placed her on a chair and carried her into a room inside the house. The small chamber was extremely simple, furnished only with a few chairs. Holy images, flanked by a few burning candles, hung on the whitewashed walls.

After courteously suggesting we make ourselves comfortable, the healer sat down beside my mother and prayed in hushed tones. I kept my eyes on my mother. Natural color gradually replaced the pallor of her face, and her body straightened and appeared charged with vitality.

After praying for about an hour, the old woman announced she was finished, and asked my mother how she felt.

"So much better than when I came in," my mother said, looking at the healer with wonderment. "I can't recall feeling so much energy." At the old woman's instruction, my mother got up and walked around the small room unassisted.

My heart burst with joy and tears trickled down my father's cheeks to witness the dramatic change in my mother's condition. It had been a long struggle, but we seemed to have won the battle. Convinced God and Jesus had answered our prayers by sending my mother's cousin to our home on the previous night and for guiding her to the kindly healer, I thanked them. Clearly, the woman was an instrument of God!

The old woman seemed satisfied with the outcome and suggested the good Lord had listened to our prayers. After a few moments of silence, she spoke directly to my father and placed the blame of my mother's illness on three women who had conspired to cast a spell on her. The healer went on to explain the techniques they had used and the sequence of events in precisely the way they had occurred, saying that without her intervention my mother would certainly have died. Then she instructed us to return to her in two weeks to receive an amulet that would protect us from those wishing to cause us harm.

My father asked the old woman her fee. She asked for 1,000 lire, which at the time was the equivalent of what a physician routinely charged for an office visit.

I asked the healer how she managed to help my mother and how she knew who had put the hex on her. She simply replied, "Mine is a gift from God." Blessing us with the sign of the cross, she granted us permission to leave, reminding us to return in two weeks.

Chapter 4

When the group congregating outside the house saw my mother come down the steps, they were incredulous. This was the same woman who one hour earlier had been brought in on a chair and who was now able to walk on her own. Their joy blended with ours, as we all realized that what had occurred was nothing short of a perfect miracle.

This event was a critical lesson for me, illustrating the importance of keeping an open mind. Had we rejected my aunt's advice based on our prejudices and ignorance, my mother would have paid with her life!

In the days following my mother's healing, I was in high spirits. It's difficult even now to express the emotions I felt seeing her restored to good health and returning to her role as woman of the house.

Two weeks later, just as the old healer had asked us, the family returned to Marsala to claim the promised amulet. The elderly healer placed the amulet in my mother's hand. "Whenever you—or anyone in your family," she said, looking around at the rest of us, "sense fear, just think or touch the amulet. Then believe with all your mind and all your heart that it will shield you from any evil influence, known or unknown." She stepped back and looked at us. "No one can hurt you." She blessed us with the sign of the cross and dismissed us.

After this event, we analyzed what the old healer had told us. To our surprise, she had been right. Accordingly, I asked myself:

- **How was my mother cured without the use of drugs?**
- **How could the healer have fathomed the reasons and conditions that had caused my mother's illness?**
- **How could she, almost instantaneously, have restored my mother's health and energy?**
- **Was she endowed with supernatural powers?**
- **If so, why did God endow only a few selected individuals with such extraordinary gifts?**
- **Why did He not give them to everyone?**

In regard to the amulet, I asked myself:
- **Did the amulet really have the power to protect us?**
- **If it did, where did its powers come from?**

Regarding the three women who were at the root of my mother's problems, I wanted to know:
- **How had they acquired the power to cause misfortune to another human being?**
- **If God were truly our creator, and the fountainhead of all goodness, love, and justice, why would He allow such awful things to happen?**
- **How could God's apparent perfection be reconciled with the imperfection and evil that fill the hearts and minds of so many men and women, all of whom were of His own creation?**
- **Why did evil, pain, misery, sorrow, dissention, and strife have to exist in this world?**
- **If God was indeed that powerful, couldn't He change the minds and souls of human beings with a simple act of His will and transform them into good and reasonable creatures?**

I could find no satisfactory answers to any of my questions—leaving me constantly vulnerable to feelings of sadness and uncertainty. Despite my youth, I instinctively felt an answer lay somewhere, and that human experiences—good and bad—were all essential and important. But the question was: why? And where could I find the answers?

CHAPTER 5
Return to School

It was already spring and my father had sown eight acres of tomatoes, my mother was doing well, and I was getting ready to go back to work at the garage. The tomatoes, which had already begun to sprout, needed constant care. My father and Gioacchino, despite their best efforts, were not able to do all the work on their own and needed to hire an extra hand.

During my mother's illness, besides having spent all our savings, we had contracted a lot of debt, which became a constant source of concern for my father. Considering the circumstances, I suggested that instead of going back to the mechanic's shop, where I was earning very little, I could help by assisting him in the fields—thereby avoiding the need to hire another helper. Only after extracting my agreement to return to the garage following the tomato harvest did my father accept my proposal. He was adamant about my learning a trade, because he was convinced doing so would ensure me a better future for my life than farming.

The tomato plants needed frequent irrigation. The river was shallow, more like a creek. A man-made channel branched from the river and provided water to the farmers along it. Unfortunately, there wasn't enough water to go around. The farmers at the beginning of the channel had the option of using it for their own needs or allowing the water to travel on down the channel to the other farms. In those days, there was no organization in place that oversaw the distribution of water. Therefore, those at the end of the channel—as we were—had to rely on our own diplomacy in talking the farmers before us into letting the water trickle all the way down. Thanks to my father's excellent efforts of diplomacy, we usually succeeded in obtaining the water we needed.

One afternoon, while we rested in the shadow of an olive tree, a cotton-growing neighbor by the name of Matteo approached us. After the customary greetings, he asked my father what he thought about the water distribution problem. My father replied that irrigating our land every night was next to impossible since other people needed water as much as we did, so we had to be satisfied with having water every four days or so.

"On this very night," Matteo said, "I will have water."

"How can you be so sure?" Father asked.

"Trust me, I will have it." His tone suggested he would not have it by negotiation.

"Matteo, Matteo," my father said. "No side ever wins through force and violence. You will always get better results through persuasion and good manners."

Matteo shook his head. "See you tonight." He hurried on his way.

That evening, as Matteo was in the channel to seize all the water available, he noticed that another farmer was using it.

Instead of approaching the man politely and asking permission to channel the water for his own use, Matteo secretly deflected the water flow to his own field, thereby preventing it from reaching its intended destination. After approximately ten minutes, the farmer noticed water was no longer flowing and investigated the problem. When he confronted Matteo and asked what he was doing, Matteo announced that for that one evening, he was going to use all the water for himself. The farmer tried to reason with him, explaining he had hired several helpers for the evening and that, whether they worked or not, he still had to pay them. Hoping for a compromise, he proposed they share the water between them. But Matteo refused, and a heated argument ensued. Both men lost control. The farmer hit Matteo with the shovel, causing a large gash on his head. With

Chapter 5

blood flowing like water, he wound up in the hospital.

My father used that occasion to address his belief in non-violence, explaining to Gioacchino and me that "reasonable human beings never seek to obtain through force what they can otherwise have through common sense and courtesy."

Had Matteo listened to his advice and adhered to these principles, he never would have wound up at the hospital, and his cotton would have gotten some measure of water. According to my father's theory, there was a solution to every problem, which could be discovered by reasoning things out calmly.

"Only when we allow pride and anger to get the upper hand," he said, "do we lose the ability to distinguish right from wrong, causing repercussions that often prove disastrous for all concerned."

I listened to my father with my mouth wide open, wondering how an illiterate farmer who had never read a book could utter such lofty words of wisdom. Despite the fact I was only fourteen at the time, his words have remained engraved in my heart and mind. I try to put his philosophy into practice every day of my life.

That year the tomato harvest was bountiful, allowing us to pay all the debts we had contracted and look forward to the future with greater hope and tranquility. But as happens more often than not, as soon as things get back on track, trouble waits around the corner. During that summer, my father's best mule began to limp, and eventually her condition worsened to the point where she could no longer walk. The veterinarian told my father on more than one occasion that according to his experience, there was no cure for what was ailing the animal. This revelation worried us a lot, as the expense of replacing our mule was quite high.

Since I had finished school at that point, I spent many of my evenings reading books. Somehow, this attenuated my sorrow for not having finished my formal studies. Although I was aware I could not return to school, every night before I fell asleep, I envisioned myself attending the Technical Institute in Sciacca.

It was already autumn, the tomato harvest was almost over, and it was time to plow the land and prepare it for sowing. In those days before modern mechanization offered effective options, the plow had to be dragged by an animal, and the mule was indispensable for the task. No longer able to depend on our old and ailing mule, my father began his quest for a new one.

October 15, 1960, was a dismal, rainy day, so we couldn't go to work in the fields. Over breakfast, my father announced it was time for me to return to the mechanic's shop and continue my apprenticeship. Resigned to my fate, I nodded. Afterward, we sought a gentleman named Carmelo who owned the service station where he sold, among other things, mechanic's overalls.

When we arrived at the store, his assistant informed us he didn't know the cost of the overalls, and that we had to ask Carmelo, who at the time, was at his olive oil processing location. The olive harvest had already started, and he was spending a lot of his time on that business. Since the place was not far from the service station, we went off in search of him. Once we found Carmelo, my father inquired if he would accompany us to the service station so we could purchase a pair of mechanic's overalls for me. Carmelo apologized for being too busy and asked that we return on the following day. Since one more day made no difference to my father, he agreed to come back.

As I will explain later, this seemingly insignificant episode turned out to be one of the most important events of my life, setting in motion those changes that would shift the direction of my future.

After leaving Carmelo, we set off to visit Zio (uncle) Lillo, who lived close by. My father wanted his brother's advice on a mule he was considering for purchase. When we arrived at Zio Lillo's home, my father asked if he would accompany him to check out the mule. Zio Lillo said he would.

After my uncle got dressed, the three of us set out for the town square. While walking, we met Mr. Salvatore Tortorici, my friend Enzo's father. I asked him how Enzo was, and he replied that his

Chapter 5

son was home with a bad cold. Upon hearing this, I asked my father permission to visit my friend, which he immediately granted.

I found Enzo in bed. "How are you feeling?"

"The worst is over," he said. "I'll be going back to school tomorrow." He sat up. "Did you hear about the new technical institute for surveyors and accountants that just opened in town?"

I moved closer. "No. Tell me about it."

"It is a private institution, not a state school."

"Oh." I knew what that meant. High tuition—at least, too high for us. "Has anyone said what the tuition is?"

"Five thousand lire a month," Enzo said. That would've been the equivalent of eight U.S. dollars. Then he said:

"Why don't you ask your father for permission to enroll?" Enzo asked.

I laughed out loud. "That's a great idea, but unfortunately a hopeless one."

"Why?"

Since we had no secrets from each other, I sat down on the side of his bed. "You know very well the financial condition of my family," I said. "And now, with the additional expense of a new mule, the notion of me going to school is virtually impossible."

Enzo shook his head. "If you really want it, it can be done."

"No—"

"Yes. Your father still gets his army pension, right? Is that not five thousand lire a month? The same amount as the monthly tuition?" I remained silent for some time. Many strange sensations flowed through my being—nervousness, fear, anxiety, joy. I knew in the deepest parts of my heart that I should follow my friend's advice. As soon as I made that decision, my fear and nervousness disappeared. I was left with a strong sense of peace and self-assurance. I couldn't wait to speak with my father and explain that I wanted to return to school and not to the mechanic's shop. I had the strange sensation that he would understand and find a way to grant me my wish.

"Well, what do you think?" Enzo asked.

After a short while I looked him straight in the eye and slowly and calmly nodded my head. "You may be right. I will talk to my father. What do I have to lose?"

With my heart filled with hope, I rushed straight home where I found my father and Zio Lillo talking. I looked at my father. "Did you get the mule?"

My father shook his head. "He's a good mule, but the price is much too high."

"One hundred sixty-five thousand lire," Zio Lillo said.

My breath left me. The euphoria I had experienced shortly before getting home gave way to fear. The cost of the mule would automatically preclude any possibility of my father being able to send me back to school.

"Do you feel all right?" my father asked.

"Yes," I said.

"You sure?"

"Yes, I'm fine," I said.

"What's bothering you?"

"Nothing."

"If it's the mule that's bothering you, stop worrying about it."

"I'm okay, Papa. Really."

He gripped one of my shoulders in each of his hands and held me close to him, his eyebrows bent in concern. "I know you too well. Something is bothering you." He let go of me, but remained close. "You know you can confide in me. And after you talk about things, you know how much better you feel." Then he smiled.

I took a deep breath. I already knew what his response would be, but I related what I had learned from Enzo Tortorici.

When I finished, he was quiet.

"I would like very much to return to school and continue my studies," I said.

My father's eyes grew large. Then, trying to find the right words

Chapter 5

to express himself, slowly and with an expression that showed all his love and at the same time sadness for not being able to say yes to my request, he reminded me of the family's financial condition—and that my going back to school was simply not possible.

"With a few sacrifices, maybe we could do it," I said. "With the money we would've spent on overalls, we can buy some of my textbooks, and those we can't afford to buy, I could probably find someone to share with me."

My father simply stared at me.

"For my tuition," I said, "we could use your war pension." It all seemed so logical to me.

A knock sounded on the front door. Two people had come to speak with my father. Feeling that their conversation would be a long one, I went for a walk in the square.

When I got home that night, my father was already in bed, so I was unable to finish my talk with him. The rest of the night I tossed in my bed imagining how nice it would be to return to school.

The rain continued through the following morning, so there would be no working in the fields. As I was about to get up, I heard the voice of Zio Lillo, who had stopped by to see if my father had decided to buy the mule.

Later, over breakfast, my father told me to get ready because we had to go buy the overalls.

"Papa," I said, "I thought about this all night long. I don't want to become a mechanic."

My father said nothing.

"If going back to school isn't possible," I said, "then I will continue working with you in the fields until I am eighteen, at which time I will join the Italian army."

"If you keep on doing farming work," he said, "in time it will be more difficult for you to do anything else. So change your clothes and come with me."

I ignored his request.

"Go do what you were told," my father said, raising his voice.

"No. I won't go with you to buy overalls." He looked at me. "Go. Now." His voice was loud.

"I do not want to be a mechanic!" I shouted.

My father moved closer to me with a raised hand, ready to slap my face. I backed up to avoid the blow.

My mother, who had been closely following our heated dialogue, rushed between us to shield me. "Calm down now," she said to my father in her soothing voice.

He lowered his raised arm, turned his weary eyes downward, and found a chair to sit upon. He sat there in silence for what seemed like a long time. During that interlude, regretful that I had angered my father, I tried to get close to him and say I was sorry. But raising his eyes and looking at me, he gestured with his hand to be quiet. I started looking at my father and noticed now his expression had changed, that he looked sad and confused—even desperate. His deep, blue eyes were veiled with tears. Never had I seen him in such a state.

Collecting himself, he went on to say in almost a whisper, as if he were speaking to himself, "Paolo, don't you know by now that no one could ever understand your plight as well as I can? Being illiterate myself, nothing would or could make me happier and prouder than to see you earn a professional diploma. But I am realistic about our financial conditions, and I fear that even if we could manage the expense for now, we wouldn't be able to continue for the full five years. Now, wouldn't it be much less disappointing if you dropped out at the beginning of the road rather than at the end?"

Seeing the painful state my father was in, I realized it was not fair of me to put him through so much turmoil. Perhaps he was right, I thought at that moment. I should follow his counsel. We remained quiet for quite some time after that.

Zio Lillo, who had been silent until then, interrupted what had become an uncomfortable situation. He said he didn't have the necessary funds; otherwise, he would be more than happy to lend us the money, allowing me to go to school.

My brother Gioacchino had observed the whole debate. "Father, please stop worrying. If Paolo really wants to continue his schooling, he should be allowed to do so."

Our father raised his head and looked at him. "What would we do if we don't have the money for Paolo to finish school?"

"As soon I am eighteen, which is only four months away, I will immigrate to Germany and will send all the money I can save home to help out the family and cover Paolo's expenses."

Surprised by his statement, we all looked at him.

Because of our reaction and expressed concerns, he smiled. We all continued to stare at him. We could not believe that at his young age, for the love of his family, he could make that big of a commitment.

After what seemed to be a long while, seeing that nobody was saying anything, my brother slowly walked to our father. "Don't worry," he said, looking into his eyes with affection. "Let Paolo go back to school. Everything will be all right."

Tears brimmed my father's eyes. He considered the situation, and then took a deep breath. "Yes, Paolo, you may enroll in school," he said. "But promise me you will undertake your studies with the utmost of seriousness and commitment. If you fail an exam, you'll never have another chance."

"I will never give you a reason to regret this. I promise," I said. "I'll do everything in my power to make sure all of you, one day in the future, will be proud of your decision."

Thus as they got on their way to go buy the mule, I, brimming with joy and enthusiasm, went to the Technical Institute to enroll in the first year of my study program.

What until a few hours before seemed only a dream had now become reality. The miracle had occurred, and the course of my life had changed.

This last experience, clearly once more, demonstrated to me that the old saying, "***VOLERE SIGNIFICA POTERE!***" *(**To Want Means To Be Able To!**)* expresses a profound truth that I was not yet fully able to comprehend.

It would take me years of study and experience to really understand its deep spiritual message and the laws that gave it meaning.

CHAPTER 6
New School

My first day of class was very exciting and filled with joy. Furthermore, in my class I found an old school mate of mine, Enzo Vella, whom I had known since the fourth grade and whose friendship was a source of great encouragement to me.

During the first few months of classes, I was able to keep my interest at a high level. Before long, however, I became aware that the school's academic standards were low, and the preparation level of its faculty left a lot to be desired. Ultimately, the students were not able to learn as they should and the situation became a source of annoyance and irritation for me. By March, Enzo and I decided to withdraw from school. With the help of two private tutors—one in math, and one in French and Italian—we prepared for the entrance examinations for the second year class at the Technical Institute in Sciacca, a fishing and industrial center twelve miles from Ribera. The Sciacca Institute was a state school and far superior to the one we had been attending.

Enzo and I had become accustomed to daily studying in a small house out in the country where no one could disturb us. As we were going over our biology text one day, we found a topic dealing with the human anatomy. Concluding that it would not be covered in our exams, we decided to skip over it, but deep inside myself, I heard a voice advising me otherwise. At first, I tried to ignore it, but the voice grew stronger, keeping me in a state of anxiety and unable to concentrate on the other subjects. I explained my feelings to Enzo. We mutually agreed to go back and study the chapter very thoroughly. After that I felt relaxed and self-assured. We continued studying.

When examination time finally arrived, the instructor asked me to sit down. He took his time considering, then finally asked me to speak about the human body. I was momentarily shocked, hardly trusting my ears. But as soon as I regained my composure, the correct answers flowed from my mind. The examiner was impressed.

On my way home, I pondered the situation. Had it been merely a coincidence, or had something deep inside my heart made me aware of the questions to be asked—thereby triggering in my mind the intention of studying that chapter on the human body? I was unable to fathom the answer.

By October, having passed the entrance exams, I was admitted to the Sciacca Technical Institute, an excellent school with first class instructors. Thus began my four years at that school, which were going to have a significant bearing on my future.

At the end of February of that year, 1961, Gioacchino immigrated to Germany, where he found work as a laborer. As promised, every month he sent home all the money he could in order to help the family.

Meanwhile, at the beginning of the school year, in order to encourage students to study with greater diligence and determination, the president of the institute announced that whoever passed the final exams with a B average or better would receive free textbooks for the following school year. I wound up qualifying for that prize every year.

The curriculum at the school consisted of two main areas, the sciences and the humanities. The former focused on mathematics, physics, chemistry, biology, and agriculture, and the latter on Italian, French, history, geography and literature. The sciences interested me more. I applied myself diligently to their study and excelled in them. Such was not the case with the humanities. I managed to pass those exams with a C average, fulfilling the requirements, but I was not the least bit interested in them. I often wondered why this was so, but I was unable to find an answer. I even asked my teachers, but they too replied they didn't know. It was a difficult phenomenon to understand or explain, they said.

The study of mathematics and physics, with all their rules and applications, was a constant source of attraction for my speculative pursuits. Applying myself to agriculture, zoology, and anatomy fulfilled my desire to understand the mechanisms of nature and to explore their interconnections and interdependencies. These ties demonstrated that all of nature basically functions in the same manner and that in order to survive, each branch of creation depends upon the other. What I found most fascinating was the study of chemistry—atomic structure, in particular. I learned that atoms are composed of particles that scientists call electrons, protons, and neutrons, which are nothing more than electrical or energy charges. Another thing I learned was that the number of electrons, protons, and neutrons constituting the atom differs in every element—giving each one a different appearance and a distinct set of characteristics.

It was almost impossible to believe that iron, gold, oxygen, hydrogen, aluminum, copper, silver, etc. that appear so different to our eyes, are in reality, made from the same particles — electrons, protons, and neutrons, and that the only difference between them is the number of electrons, protons, and neutrons contained in their atoms.

What particularly fascinated me was:
- **When the atoms come in contact with one another, they can exchange their electrons, protons, and neutrons—giving rise to new atoms.**
- **The atoms can regroup with one another, creating molecules.**
- **The molecules can regroup, thus creating substances, which, in turn, create the universe.**

Thus, I concluded that everything I learned from the study of chemistry demonstrated that Creation is nothing but an infinite mass of atoms grouped together whose very essence is energy. Therefore it follows that all Creation is simply condensed energy.

In the process of assimilating these notions, I became convinced that every day I spent in school was a new milestone in my life. The benefits I reaped from both books and lectures were a growing source of fulfillment. And every day I appreciated my brother and my parents' sacrifices and their willingness to allow me to continue my studies.

CHAPTER 7
First Love

While I was attending the Technical School for Surveyors in Ribera, I made friends with Mario, a student from a small town twelve miles from Ribera. One Sunday afternoon, my two friends, Giuseppe Zabbara and Enzo Tortorici, and I traveled to Mario's hometown, where we met in the town piazza. After the customary exchange of greetings, he invited us to the local pastry shop, then home to meet his family. His parents and brother were warm, delightful people who, in those first few moments, made us feel right at home. When his sister Giannina walked into the room and I looked into her eyes, I felt something I had never experienced. Her way of speaking, her captivating smile, and her charming simplicity evoked a kind of inner feminine beauty and serenity that I had often fantasized to find in the girl who would one day become my life companion.

After chatting with the family for a while, Giuseppe, Enzo, and I took our leave, but on the way back to Ribera, I felt nervous—unable to keep the image of Giannina out of my mind. That night I couldn't sleep—thoughts of her occupied my mind. At first I dismissed my feelings as no more than infatuation, but the more time went by, the more urgent became my longing.

Seeing Giannina again would not be easy. The fact that she was the sister of a good friend of mine complicated the issue, since the bond of friendship for me is one of the purest and noblest of sentiments existing between two human beings. I feared that if Mario were to find out how I felt about Giannina, he would misinterpret my intentions and become offended, which could have severely compromised our friendship.

During the Christmas holidays, Giuseppe, Enzo and I went to visit Mario in his hometown. After I saw Giannina again I had no doubts about my feelings anymore, I knew with certainty I was completely in love with her—and was more convinced than ever that she possessed all the attributes of the girl of my dreams, the one who would one day become my wife.

In those days, particularly in that part of the world, young people did not enjoy the liberties they do now. So whenever Giannina and I had a chance to see each other, we were surrounded by her relatives, making it impossible for me to declare my feelings.

Finally, after two interminable years of waiting, Giannina came to study in Ribera. One day, after rallying all my courage, I went to see her. "Giannina," I said. Her name, as beautiful as she, rolled easily off my tongue.

She smiled.

My heart soared. "I don't know how to say this, so I'll just say it." I filled my lungs with air and said, "Giannina, I love you, and when I am with you I am the happiest young man in the entire world. I know that I'm young and you're young, but I'm sure of my feelings, and I know that with you at my side, I will find the happiness every human being seeks."

She listened, her smile losing only the tiniest bit of its luster. "I'm sorry," she said. "I'm not ready."

"Ready? There's nothing to be—"

"I'm too young to be tied down. I'm not ready."

"Giannina, please," I said. "Think about it. Don't give me your answer now."

"I'm sorry, Paolo. I'm quite sure of my feelings."

"Is there someone else? Is that the problem?"

"No. There's no one else."

"Then think about it. That's all I ask."

Chapter 7

"I care about you as a friend, Paolo. But that's all." She looked deep into my eyes, her dark eyes shadowed. "And I want to continue to be your friend."

I nodded, my throat tight. "Yes. Of course. We will always be friends."

Then we said goodbye.

The fact that she was not involved emotionally with anyone and was concerned about our friendship gave me a glimmer of hope that in time she might change her mind.

A few days after this episode, a friend saw her with another fellow. Soon after, I discovered that not only had she been meeting with him on occasion, but she was in love with him. I was devastated. After having waited and hoped for so long, my dreams were suddenly shattered. What I found particularly difficult to accept was Giannina's lack of sincerity.

My mind was filled with one simple question:

Why hadn't she simply told me the truth—that she was in love with someone else?

This experience caused me to suffer far more than I could have imaged and inspired me to develop a great desire to understand life in general.

More questions flooded my thinking:
- **What is the reason for living?**
- **What is the true essence of life?**
- **What is the law that governs human existence?**

I thought that if I could even begin to grasp the answers to these questions, I would find some peace of mind. From that moment on, I began to observe the people with whom I came into contact—attempting to understand what they were thinking, what they were doing, and the reason for their actions. What I discovered filled my heart with sadness. Perhaps for the first time in my life, I noticed that in all strata of society some people, at times, were egocentric, hypocritical, and thought only of themselves. I discovered that often respect for others was based not on the nobility of one's soul or character, but on socioeconomic considerations such as money, family background, and political and societal influence.

Particularly I noted with sorrow that the poorest and least clever were among the most humiliated, oppressed, and ignored members of society. The cunning always seemed ready to pounce on the innocent; the wicked took advantage of the good without concern for any psychological or physical harm they might cause.

In observing the animal kingdom, I noticed they had the same problems. Indeed, some animals seek dominance of its group—and sometimes, they draw upon all their cunning to achieve their goals.

I observed that animals usually kill to nourish themselves, but man will often not only kill for food, but also for the pleasure of killing, for power, and for ideology. How many wars have been and continue to be waged in the name of God? Every century offers more than one glaring example.

So I asked myself: Were those actions justifiable?

Furthermore, in observing the human species in connection with the animal and vegetable kingdoms, I noticed the kingdoms were dependent upon one another for their survival. From my school studies I had already learned that the reproductive and biological process of humans, animals, and plants are similar and all are affected by disease—and are not immune to suffering, leading me to conclude that nature—including man—is in a constant battle with itself leading nowhere.

So again I asked myself: Why?

According to some Biblical teachings, pain is a punishment devised by God for Adam and Eve's disobedience.

Then I asked myself:

- **If pain is the result of a quarrel between man and God, why**

are animals made to suffer as humans? Is God punishing them, as well—and why?
- What about the vegetable kingdom that clothes and nourishes every species on the planet? What have they done that would justify their diseases?
- How can God, assuming that He exists, allow such confusion and injustice to take place?
- Would a good and loving God sanction evil, pain, disease and suffering? I thought not.
- Why, then, do they exist?

I asked myself more questions:
- Who is God in His true essence?
- What does He look like?
- Where does He reside?
- How can He be contacted?
- Why have I never heard of anyone seeing or speaking with Him?
- Why does He not manifest Himself from time to time so everyone can believe in Him—assuming He's a "Him"?

These notions led me to pose more questions:
- What is the true purpose of life?
- What is the reason for suffering and death?
- What happens to us after death?
- Does another life system exist elsewhere in the universe?
- Is there a Heaven and Hell as commonly believed?
- Considering the affinities that exist among humans, animals and plants, why do we believe in some form of afterlife for humans, but not for plants and animals?
- If the body of a man is cremated, aren't his ashes similar to those of trees and fellow animals?

Then I asked:
- **Does life end in nothingness?**
- **And if it does end in nothingness, why live it?**
- **What is the difference between dying at eighteen or nineteen years of age and dying at eighty or ninety?**
- **Why are all living beings subject to disease?**
- **How does disease originate?**

Where could I find the answers to my queries and get relief from all the depressing problems making my life miserable?

Since I could find no answers, I fell into a long period of depression. My studies suffered and I got to the point where I lost the will to live. Thoughts of suicide permeated my mind. Whenever I fell into such a deep pit, something inside me made me recall the love of my parents and brothers, and the sacrifices they were making in order to send me to school. I thought also about my brother Gioacchino, who was still working in Germany and sending home all his savings for my sake, just as he had promised. I remembered the vow I had made to never disappoint or delude them.

These considerations counterbalanced my thoughts of suicide. I could not help but worry about the profound repercussions such a selfish act would have on my family. It would break their hearts, and no amount of time could ever extinguish their sorrow.

On top of it all, would not such a deed demonstrate cynicism and egoism? Were not these the very human characteristics I hated most? How could I even consider putting them into practice by ending my own life?

After those periods of anxiety and self-doubt, I simply concluded I had no right to betray my family's trust in me. Even if it were my own life with which I was dealing, I still had the responsibility to respect their feelings and keep the promises I had made. I forced myself to stop thinking about the problems that were torturing me and concentrated instead on those projects for which I had a responsibility and obligation to fulfill.

Chapter 7

I noticed that the less my mind was occupied with negativity, the greater became my desire to succeed and do well in my studies. As if by some strange and powerful enchantment I drew myself out of this depression, and managed to pass all my final examinations with good grades.

Due to my overwhelming need to understand life, I rode this emotional roller coaster until my early thirties, when I discovered the process and the techniques through which I found the answers to my questions.

CHAPTER 8
First Trip to Germany

One day during the 1963-64 school year, I told my father I wanted to visit my brother in Germany during the summer recess. I suggested I could work there and earn some money to defray school expenses for the following year. He replied that if I passed the final exams with a "B" average or better and received free books as a reward for my good grades, then I would have his permission to go. I gladly accepted his challenge—convinced, of course, that I would prevail.

Since childhood, whenever I saw planes soar through the skies or bus loads of tourists pass through our town, I dreamed that someday I would be able to travel far beyond my little town of Ribera. Now that I had the opportunity of making my dream come true, I felt so charged with energy that I fell into a state of near euphoria. That year, motivated by the thought of going to Germany, I applied myself to my studies with greater concentration than normal, achieving excellent results in the process.

Three days after school closed for the summer, I received my final examination results. As expected, my grades were above a "B" average. I could hardly wait for the moment my father would come home from work. I waited impatiently at the front door of my house, looking down the street from where he would be arriving. As soon as I saw him riding his mule, I ran towards him with the good news. "Get your suitcases ready," he said, his smile indicating his pride.

That evening I wrote to my brother informing him of my good grades and of my planned arrival date in Germany. I was thoroughly elated at the thought of traveling the whole of Italy by train through its most beautiful, renowned cities: Napoli, Roma, Firenze, and Milano, and then crossing Switzerland before finally reaching Germany, where I would be able to embrace my brother. The idea of seeing him, meeting new people and observing their customs thrilled me.

One week later, with two packed suitcases and accompanied by my parents, my brother Ignazio, my closest friends, and a few neighbors, I headed for the bus stop to catch the bus for Palermo. It was the first time I had ever left my home and family. Although the idea of the trip filled me with joy, when I said goodbye to my folks and friends, I knew I would miss them all.

A few hours after catching the bus, I arrived at the railroad station in Palermo and boarded the train for Germany. As the train pulled away, I stared out the window, attempting to impress on my memory everything within my line of vision.

The railroad track leading from Palermo to Messina ran exactly along the seacoast, a few yards from the water's edge. From my window, I could behold the vast stretch of sea, where vacationers in motorboats enjoyed the water. The beaches were crowded with countless umbrellas and small tents creating a variegated pattern vaguely resembling an unfinished mosaic.

Looking inland, the countryside along the coast was almost entirely covered with a blanket of citrus groves, orchards, flowers and vegetables—all flooded by the sun's bright, golden rays. In spite of a fresh breeze coming in from the sea, the air was steeped in the fragrance of flowers and wild herbs, blending with the scent of ripe fruit. Far away on the horizon, sea and sky merged in an enchanting blend of blue—conjuring a spellbinding, unforgettable tableau.

Reaching the Straits of Messina, I was astonished to see the enormous ferry—loaded with trains, cars and passengers—plowing the deep, blue waters. I had never been on a ship, and as soon as my coach was loaded, I proceeded inside. Spurred by curiosity, I roamed around, wondering about the size and power of a ship capable of hauling such an enormous load. The crossing lasted about two hours, and then the train continued along its course towards Naples, Rome, Florence, and Milan.

When the conductor announced our imminent arrival at the Eternal City, I wondered whether I was dreaming or truly living out my fantasy of seeing Rome—if only from a train. The landscapes I saw northward were simply beautiful and completely different from what I had been used to in Sicily during summer. Whereas on our island from June onwards everything became parched due to the absence of rainfall and the summer heat, the fields here were green and covered with wild flowers.

Upon reaching Switzerland, I was awestruck by its beautiful mountain settings and rich streams thundering down from steep heights—perfectly visible and audible from the train. Cows peacefully grazing in green meadows inspired in me a deep sense of serenity. I felt like I was dreaming. In the course of a relatively short period of time, that train had transported me into a completely different new world.

After a stretch of about thirty-six hours, I finally reached Offenburg, the city where Gioacchino lived at the time. He and two of his buddies were waiting for me at the railroad station. I was overjoyed to see him again, and after the customary greetings, we all proceeded to their dwelling—which, to my surprise, was not a house but a railroad car.

"Like my home?" Gioacchino asked.

I was speechless.

He laughed. "The German government provides these for those working on the railroad." He showed me around. Some coaches served as sleeping quarters, others as kitchens and dining areas, and still others as toilets and showers. For the workers, immigrants for the most part, this was considered home.

My disappointment forced me to alter my thinking about the kind of life led abroad by Italian immigrants. I had imagined them to be quite comfortable. How wrong I was! Having seen their living conditions, I was now eager to scrutinize the rest of their

Chapter 8

environment and the sort of life they led.

A few days after arriving in Offenburg, with help from Gioacchino, I landed a job at a shipping company.

The work was hard, and because my muscles were not used to such physical exertion, I was exhausted. But what affected me even more than fatigue was frustration over the language barrier, which was rendering me incapable of utilizing my capabilities to the fullest. On the job I was often treated as a child—or, worse yet, as mentally challenged—simply because I could not communicate in German. At times this inconvenience amused me, but more often it was a source of embarrassment and humiliation. I pondered my brother's situation so I would better understand the kind of obstacles he had been facing during these years of hard labor in a foreign country, and away from his loved ones.

I noticed that immigrants were often called upon to perform the most grueling and menial of jobs and were frequently humiliated—sometimes even looked upon as inferior human beings. If that were true, though, why did millions of people leave behind their families, their homes, and their land in order to immigrate? And if their plight were so unbearable, why didn't they go back home?

I discovered why. The love they bore for their families was far greater than any sacrifice they could take on. Their personal sacrifice provided their loved ones with something that otherwise would not have been available to them, such as education or a roof over their heads. Knowing they had made a significant difference in the lives of someone they loved got them past the loneliness, the sadness, and the aching muscles.

The images that impressed me the most—and those that I still prize as the most important of my German experiences—came into view every evening, when the laborers came back from work. As soon as they arrived, they hurried to the post office for mail distribution.

While waiting for their names to be called, their facial expressions shifted from anxiety, to hope, to joy or to sadness. As each man opened his mail, he would turnaround and slowly, almost hypnotically—without taking his eyes off his letter—proceed toward his coach. The faces of each of these men took on different expressions. Some radiated joy, others sadness—but all of them, regardless of how they reacted, had a gleam in their eyes, or, more often than not, tear-stained cheeks. Those who had not received mail walked slowly toward their coach—their heads bowed in disappointment.

The sight of those men demonstrated the harshness of their lives, and for the majority of them, mail call constituted one of the most beautiful, important, and sometimes painful moments of their exhausting day. News from home was what gave them the strength to carry on with their lives.

At the same time I was weighing the plight of the immigrants, I also noticed that the German people were very well-mannered and respectful, and enjoyed a standard of living far superior to that of most Sicilians. Young people, for example, enjoyed much greater freedom and independence. On weekends they were permitted to go out dancing and having fun with their friends—something that wasn't even dreamed of in my native Ribera at that time. Another thing I couldn't help noticing was that the majority of Germans, besides being good workers, were endowed with a creative spirit. Most things they did were accomplished with the utmost of diligence and to the limit of their capabilities. What struck me the most, however, was their dynamism—their meticulousness and professionalism in whatever they did, thus assuring their industries and employers a great degree of success. Such an outlook—virtually nonexistent in my native Sicily—gave me a new perspective as I began to appreciate its correlation to the degree of success we attain in life—whether as individuals, companies, or nations.

CHAPTER 9
Trip to Ribera

Weeks fled by. It was suddenly mid-September, and I was committed to returning to Ribera by October 1 in order to finish my last year of school. The thought of going back home and seeing my parents, whom I had missed very much, filled me with happiness, but I felt sad at the thought of leaving Gioacchino alone in Germany. My emotions were tearing me apart.

As the train started slowly moving out of the station, and I waved to my brother, I couldn't help thinking how deep his love was for me and for the rest of the family. He was sacrificing the best years of his youth for our sake. Deep in my heart grew a great sense of veneration for him, which remains unchanged even today. On that return trip to Sicily I was no longer animated by the same enthusiasm I had felt when I was going to Offenburg a few months earlier. Now I was looking out of the window, disillusioned and indifferent—downcast at the thought of my brother being left alone. I didn't feel right in leaving him behind, but what could I do?

During that moment of sadness I conceived the idea that one day, in the future, I would gather my family together in one place, and I vowed to myself I would never stop trying until I fulfilled that pledge.

When the train reached Milan, I took advantage of the stopover to visit the DUOMO, the third largest church in Europe, which was as magnificent as I had imagined. Then I went on to Florence, where some friends and former neighbors from Ribera were waiting at the train station. They had moved a few years before to Campi Bisenzio, a town near Florence. I stayed with them for a week, during which they took me all around Florence and gave me a chance to visit the city's great monuments as well as some of the priceless art treasures known throughout the world, such as il Davide di Michelangelo's, la Cattedrale di Santa Maria del Fiore, the fourth largest church of Europe, Ponte Vecchio, with all its boutiques situated over the river Arno, and il Palazzo Vecchio, situated in Piazza della Signoria with all its status and sculptures.

From Florence I proceeded to Genova, where I met my Aunt Lina—Uncle Lillo's wife—who was visiting with her son and brother. I had only one day to appreciate that beautiful city's most important sights, like the seaport, la Torre della Lanterna, la Piazza De Ferrari, the seacoast village of Boccadasse, and the beautiful Palazzo Ducale.

At five the next afternoon, accompanied by my aunt, I boarded the train for Sicily.

As the train headed south, my mind followed its own chaotic course, recollecting memories. I analyzed my attributes and what I valued most in life. Since childhood I had a tendency to respect people of all ages not in accordance with their appearance or what they pretended to be, but by their intrinsic traits.

My predilection was for humble, honest individuals—those who were not pompous or overbearing. At the time, young people in my hometown were divided into social groups based on the socio-economic position of their families. This sort of caste system was adhered to by most of the youth and adults in our town.

In spite of my status as a student, I did not abide by the unwritten rules of the town's social canons and found my friends wherever I chose. Besides my inner circle of student pals, I had friends among young shepherds, farmers, and apprentices. I offered friendship to any youth or adult—independent of their occupation or status—as long as he or she was honest and altruistic. I simply detested egotistic and pretentious people.

My unique outlook on social rapport made it possible for me to develop a deep friendship with two particular boys, Giuseppe Zabbara

Chapter 9

and Enzo Tortorici. I grew up with them and developed a relationship so strong and sincere that even now, thirty-eight years after leaving Ribera, my bond with them is stronger than ever. Now at age sixty, I realize that rather than friends, they are like brothers to me.

The three of us had different personalities, but we all shared the same profound affection and respect for one another. Without any doubt the brightest was Enzo. Short in stature and endowed with a sharp intelligence, he became one of the top students in our class. Extremely sensitive, he spoke only when necessary, and then very little. But he was always ready to give all he had for the sake of our friendship.

Giuseppe and I were not as bright, but in contrast to Enzo, we liked to talk, a trait that made it possible for us to make a lot of friends. Giuseppe was very sturdy for his age, and with his dark complexion, he gave the false impression that he was tough. In reality, he was very tenderhearted. From the time he was a child, Giuseppe wrote poetry, which, if he were ever to publish, might be worthy of recognition. Among the three of us, I was perhaps the least gifted. But then, whenever the rare conflict arose among us, I was the one capable of settling our differences, thereby further strengthening our bond. To us, friendship was one of the most beautiful and noblest of sentiments—never to be used for personal gain, but as an end in itself. Young as we were, we created a personal philosophy of life in which sincerity, loyalty, altruism, and respect for others—especially our own parents and older people in general—were of paramount importance.

We always hung out together. Wherever one of us went, the other two followed. If, for example, one of us was invited to a party, he took along the other two. Since everyone knew how close we were, we were all always welcomed as a group. If we decided to go to the movies and one of us didn't have the money to buy a ticket, whoever did have the money paid for the other—or, if we pooled our money and it didn't add up to the price of three tickets, then no one went to the movies. We simply walked around the town piazza, where sometimes we met schoolmates of mine from nearby towns.

Good manners demanded that I invite these acquaintances to the local bar for a coffee. If Enzo or Giuseppe got the drift that I didn't have enough money to pay for everybody, one or the other would pass me money on the sly, making it appear that I was paying and letting me take credit for the treat. And since I wasn't working and never had much to spend, that scenario played out quite often. Furthermore, they never wanted their money back. What mattered to them was that I didn't look cheap in front of my schoolmates.

Now, could there have been a deeper and a more sincere sense of friendship than that?

As I looked out the window of the train, more thoughts flashed through my mind about my friends. The years were rolling by and each of us was following the road that our circumstances allowed: I was going to school; Giuseppe alternated between farming and masonry work; and Enzo had dropped out of school and worked with his father operating farming machinery.

One of the most important ideals we shared was to someday find a girl who would love us for what we were and not what we could offer in terms of luxuries and riches, although we hoped to set up a strong economic base for our families and ourselves. It would never have occurred to us to make our fortune by marrying into a wealthy family, nor to use any dishonest methods for achieving our goals. Our intention was to secure our future by putting our talents and skills to work. We were aware even then that money wasn't the key element to attaining what is commonly called "happiness," but we believed that without decent financial autonomy, the prospect of leading a reasonably comfortable and happy existence looked bleak.

In the meantime, my aunt observed me and saw me as serious and thoughtful. She asked if something was bothering me. Attempting a casual smile, I told her not to worry—everything was fine. She took that moment to tell me to eat a sandwich that she had prepared prior to our departure from Genova, putting an end to my reveries.

Chapter 9

After approximately thirty-six hours of travel, my aunt and I finally reached Ribera, and once again I was able to embrace my parents, younger brother, and all my friends and relatives.

From left: Enzo Tortorici, Enzo Vella, Paolo, brother Ignazio, Giuseppe Zabbara, Giacomo at Seccagrande the home town beach, Ribera 1963.

Paolo at Seccagrande, the home town beach, Ribera 1963.

CHAPTER 10
Graduation – Lessons from My Parents

Soon thereafter, I began my last year of school, which ended on July 26, 1965. Having successfully passed all my final exams, I was awarded a diploma for expertise in agriculture and as a land surveyor—an event that filled the hearts of my parents and brothers with great pride.

In the days following this important milestone in my life, I went to the beach practically on a daily basis. There, lying in the sun, I tried to release all the nervous tension I had accumulated during the last months in school. Later in the day, upon returning home, I often found my mother looking sad. Whenever I asked what was troubling her, she would assure me with a smile nothing was wrong.

Finally, one day her heart opened up and she confided to me. In a whisper, as if talking to herself, she said how nice it would be if the whole family could live under the same roof. I immediately caught on that she was referring to my brother Gioacchino and that she missed him terribly. I assured her that in the future, God willing, we would certainly be settled somewhere together.

A few days later while I was helping my father on the farm, I told him about that conversation. After reflecting a while and drawing a deep sigh, he gave a nod of approval, indicating that he shared my mother's view. It became all the more apparent to me how much family meant to my parents.

This led me to analyze and reflect on their lives and attitudes.

My father hadn't married my mother until he was twenty-nine. The reason he didn't marry earlier was because he had to help his parents set

*Paolo with cousin Padre Alfonzo Tortorici on the day of his ordination, brother Gioacchino and cousin Gerolamo Scaturro.
Ribera, 1965.*

Chapter 10

aside enough money for his sisters' dowries. Back then in Ribera there was no work available for girls, so if parents wanted their daughters or sisters to marry well, other members of the family were called upon to provide for the marriage settlement. That usually consisted of a house and trousseau, plus money for the wedding celebrations. If those conditions were not met, it was difficult for a young lady to find a decent husband.

After marrying my mother, my father never neglected the love and respect he had for his own parents and family. Instead, he enlarged the sphere of his affections to include my mother's parents—my grandparents Antonina and Paolo—as well as to their relatives. In order to make us children understand our father's love for family, from time to time my mother would regale us with stories.

For example, just after my parents got married, my grandmother Antonina became ill. Unfortunately, the doctors in our town could neither diagnose nor treat her ailment and gave her only a short time to live. My grandfather Paolo, as a last resort, took her to a private clinic in Palermo, where a specialist examined her and said she could be cured, adding that the treatment would be very costly. Since medical insurance was unheard of in those days, upon hearing what the costs amounted to, my grandmother told the doctor they couldn't afford the treatment. Then, turning to my grandfather, she asked to be taken back home. My grandfather looked at the doctor and told him to pay no attention to what he had heard and to start the treatment immediately. He turned to my grandmother and told her not to worry, as he would go back home to sell their house and thus be able to pay the doctor bills. He then traveled back to Ribera.

Once he got home, he related to my father and mother what he had told the doctor, remarking that he had to sell his house as soon as possible. My father said he did not have to do that—he would provide for their financial needs. Extremely touched, my grandfather embraced him with tears in his eyes, expressing his gratitude. Approximately a month later my grandmother returned home, cured of her illness.

Following that experience, my grandparents looked upon my father as a son rather than son-in-law.

In those days, my grandparent's greatest preoccupation was their daughter Carmela, who was still single and lived in Waterbury, Connecticut. In 1949, after seeking the advice of my mother and father, they decided to join my Aunt Carmela in the United States with the intention of getting her married and properly settled. They applied to the U.S. Consulate in Palermo to get the necessary visas.

After examining their applications, however, the immigration office chose to grant a visa only to my grandmother, refusing it to my grandfather, since according to their records he was a member of the Communist Party. My grandfather tried to explain that the whole thing was a terrible mistake, but the immigration officer insisted that unless he demonstrated that he was not a Communist, the consulate would be unable to issue the visa.

Unaware of how long the appeal process would take, he advised my grandmother to leave by herself and assured her he would follow as soon as he could. Reluctantly, she left for the United States, where she immediately became ill again and died thirty days after her arrival. This was a painful experience. Now that my grandmother was dead, my grandfather lost his desire to go to the U.S. He remained with us in Ribera until his own death on October 10, 1955.

During the last years of his life, my grandfather often advised my parents to encourage Aunt Carmela to file a petition with the U.S. Immigration Office so the entire family could settle in the United States, where he thought we would have a better future. But they refused, insisting they would never abandon him in the old country.

A few months before he died, my grandfather said that if my parents promised after his death, they would do everything possible to join Aunt Carmela in the U.S., he would die in peace.

A month after my grandfather's death, my mother followed through on her promise to him. She asked Aunt Carmela to petition for our admission into the U.S., which she did without hesitation.

Chapter 10

Unfortunately, during that period the American government had cut down on the quota of immigrants, and our petition was put on hold for an indefinite period. In the interim, we were forced to remain in Ribera.

My father never smoked, nor did he go to the movies, play cards or drink alcohol, except for an occasional glass of wine. All his life was dedicated to work and family. For him, family was not limited to members of the immediate household, but to nephews and nieces, as well as friends. Whenever one of them was sick or had problems, he would never fail to visit and offer words of hope and encouragement. By observing his behavior, I was able to understand the meaning of altruistic love, in which the primary aim is to bring comfort and joy into the hearts and lives of others. My father always worried about other people, never about himself, and always with the greatest of tact and sensitivity. He gave whatever he could without asking for anything in return.

In the evenings, we waited for him to get back from the fields so we could all eat together. During supper, he would tell us about what had happened at work and how he approached and resolved his problems—making us indirect participants in his daily life. He shared with us all his joys—and often his problems—demonstrating that everything he gave us was the result of much hard work and personal sacrifice.

He often took us boys out to help him in the fields so we would learn what manual labor really meant. When on Sundays Mother gave us our allowance to go out, he would tactfully remind us how much hard work had been put into earning that money and encouraged us to spend it intelligently.

When discussing the value of money, he explained it was made for our use and not the other way around. What he was trying to make us understand was that it was okay to work hard to earn money and to spend it wisely, but that it was just as important not to get too attached to it—that if we put money ahead of everything else, we were going to lose sight of the true value of life.

Materialism and egotism, although useful in achieving certain life goals, are not significant in the long run, because they invariably end up creating more problems than good things. Money, power, and self-importance do not guarantee happiness, but instead can destroy peace of mind.

Whenever he discussed such issues, he was trying to put material things into proper perspective for us in preparation for our adult lives. Peace, unity, and the well-being of our family were what interested him the most and what he tried to inculcate in our hearts and minds.

Our father always reminded us boys that there should never be envy among us; that we should always love and help one another, and that unity creates strength—one of the most important goals for which we could aim.

When peace, unity, and understanding reign within the family and there is unconditional love and support, it becomes easier to tackle and overcome most of life's problems and to reach goals. Through his own example, Father inspired us with his ideals, since he practiced what he preached.

Mother loved our father very much and shared his ideals in every aspect and the couple identified themselves as a single person, a single ideal, and a single will.

Upon analyzing all the above, I understood the great value the family represented for my parents—how we children occupied the first place in their lives, and how their love for us had no bounds. Remembering all of these things now, I realize how lucky I am to have had parents like them, as throughout my life they gave me a matchless example to emulate.

After all these considerations, I was bound to ask myself the following:

- **What kind of relationship existed among us?**
- **What did my parents mean to me?**
- **How deep was my love for them?**

Chapter 10

Our relationship was simple—and yet very deep. For example, we were not in the habit of expressing our affection in words, as so many people do. As children we were taught good manners, courtesy, honesty, and to associate only with good boys. We were taught through examples and proverbs and through common sense and persuasion whenever possible. But if kind words did not produce the desired effect, our parents did not hesitate to act firmly and, if necessary, harshly. I will always remember fondly the first and only time I tried to disobey my father.

More than my brothers, I had a tendency at times to rebel and not pay attention to what I was told. I was also vindictive. For example, if another child did me wrong, I was sure to repay him promptly, and usually more severely. It was my way of making sure he would never repeat what he had done. Because of this trait and of my rather introverted character, the other children not only left me in peace, but also tended to respect and even like me.

One day I came home from school and found my mother sick in bed and my father home from the fields. After eating, I went outside to play with the other kids in the neighborhood. I don't remember why, but I had a quarrel with another child and beat him up. When the boy's mother saw me, she ran toward me ready to whip me. But I ran away. Frustrated by her inability to catch me, she called me "figlio di puttana" (a son-of-a-prostitute). I responded that she was the "puttana" (prostitute), not my mother. She was the one climbing into bed with strangers while her husband worked abroad.

Deeply offended and angry by the truth, she tried to grab for me, but I was too fast for her. Finally, unable to reach me, she ran to my house, and yelling with rage, informed my father I had beaten up her son and called her a whore.

Observing the scene from a distance, I tried to explain to him why I had uttered such foul language. My father ordered me to be quiet and to get in the house immediately.

Figuring that I would get a sound beating, I refused to move. He repeated his command, but again I refused. By now he was irritated and ran after me. I managed to keep out of his reach. With a forbidding voice, he made it clear that since sooner or later I would have to go home, the affair would be settled then and there. Turning to the boy's mother, he excused himself for what had happened, promising her it would never happen again.

He then went into the house. By the time it got dark, I had no choice but to return home. My father waited, belt in hand. I tried to escape, but I had entered the courtyard, which was a dead end. With no way out, my father subjected me to the worst beating of my life, while reprimanding me for having disobeyed him—and warning me to never do it again.

From her sickbed, my mother heard my screams. Still wearing her nightdress, she came to my rescue, pulling me free from my father's hands. Although these days such physical action on the part of a parent would be interpreted as child abuse, that beating from my father was without a doubt the most profitable and miraculous cure I could have received for the tempering of my explosive disposition and the shaping of my character.

The following day, my father called me aside and asked how I felt. I replied that I was well. He asked if I understood why I had gotten thrashed. I answered that I should not have disobeyed him. He nodded, saying that if I had done what he had ordered in the first place, nothing would have happened. Then he went on to relate a little story that was to serve as a parable.

He explained that in the early years of a tree's growth, they have a tendency to become warped. In order to overcome this problem, farmers shore them up with sticks, since once they lignify, they can no longer be straightened. Little boys, he added, are like small trees. They need to have their character strengthened and their bad habits eliminated—and it's a father's duty to see that proper methods are applied so that children develop into respectful, obedient, honest, and responsible human beings. Then, asking for a hug, he held me tightly,

Chapter 10

telling me—a very rare occurrence, indeed—how much he loved me.

At that very moment, having allayed my fears, I realized that my father was perfectly right, and I felt for him a deep sense of love, respect, and unconditional trust. Even today, so many years after his death, those feelings have not diminished in the least. I shall always be grateful to him for his teachings, and I thank the Lord for having given me a father like him.

CHAPTER 11
In Love Again and Future Plans

I spent the summer of 1965 helping my father in the fields with the cotton harvest. Time was flying and autumn was already around the corner. Most of my classmates had already enrolled at the University of Palermo, to continue their studies.

Gioacchino wrote from Germany advising me to do the same thing, assuring me that he would cover the tuition fees, just as he had done until then. I wrote back thanking him for his offer, but I had no intention of spending another four years in a university. I was lying; I would have liked nothing better than to obtain a university degree—but I felt that I should in no way impose on my family any longer by letting them go through another four years of hardship and privation on my account. I thought they had already contributed enough by allowing me to get a professional diploma that would surely pave the way to a reasonably secure future.

It occurred to me that I could utilize the four years I'd spend going to the university to start a business that would provide economic security for me, my brothers and my parents—thereby providing a way of keeping the family together. I believed that by so doing I could somehow repay them for the sacrifices they had incurred on my behalf. But I soon concluded that no one can ever repay his or her parents and family—not only for the material goods they provide, but also for the ideals they sow in our hearts. All we can do is to love them with the same simplicity and sincerity they loved us.

Today, as the father of three sons, I realize how true that statement is, and I am more aware than ever of the important role that family

Chapter 11

plays in the life of every human being.

Did I have the capability, the strength, the courage and determination to bring such a project to completion?

I did not know the answers, and the only way to find out was to try.

I looked at the future with trust and hope.

In my moments of weakness and doubt I often recalled the Alfieri saying:

"VOLERE SIGNIFICA POTERE!" (To Want Means To Be Able To!)

And so, I asked myself what I could and would like to do.

The diploma I had just obtained allowed me to do the following:

- **Teach at the intermediate level or in a technical institute.**
- **Practice independently as an agricultural consultant and as a surveyor.**
- **Find an office job at a governmental institution.**

I examined the first possibility—teaching. At that time in Sicily there were very few posts available for teachers. So if I wanted to pursue that profession, the only choice I had was to move to northern Italy, where there were more chances of being employed. The thought of becoming a school teacher, however, did not excite me in the least. I could only foresee a constant monotony that would last for the rest of my life. Furthermore, leaving my hometown and family would not have been conducive to attaining the goal I had in mind—creating a family enterprise to keep everybody close by.

The second possibility was more to my liking; nevertheless, I was acutely aware that in my hometown there simply wasn't sufficient work in the field of agricultural consulting to support a business full time. Finding work at a governmental institution was not easy since there were very few jobs and an enormous number of applicants. These conditions had given rise to a bureaucratic machine and a corrupt frame of mind on the part of almost everyone concerned—and it worried me.

The passing of competitive exams for jobs was not based upon an individual's intelligence, capabilities, or academic preparation, but on the type of recommendations he or she could obtain. So in order to get a job, an applicant was required to actively participate in the local or regional political mechanisms. Even then, it might take years to get the sought-after position. In fact, long before the competitive examinations were held, everyone knew who would get the jobs, thus debasing the tests to a simple farce, a deception, and a waste of time. As a result, most positions in the public sector were assumed by assorted incompetents and those who lacked in training—as well as by presumptuous nincompoops who upon reaching positions of authority and power, viewed themselves as nothing less than demigods.

This state of affairs not only diminished the expertise and quality of services offered by local government, but it dampened the enthusiasm and desire on the part of students to perform well in school. Why study, after all, when all you needed was a good recommendation? Ultimately, the degree of incompetence and corruption grew exponentially.

This situation thoroughly disgusted me. I could not help but think the whole system was unfair to those young people whose families had neither the contacts nor the friends to help secure a job. The system was also cruel to the student's families, who despite their sacrifices for the sake of their children's education ended up seeing them go jobless or having to immigrate to the north in order to secure work.

Was that fair?

The thought of making plans for my future overwhelmed me. All these factors notwithstanding, I realized that in time I was bound to find a solution to my problems. I would simply wait for developments to take shape. But the first thing I had to do was complete my compulsory military service.

At the time, I was nineteen. During the Christmas holidays of 1965, I was invited to a dance, where I met a pretty, unpretentious girl named Luisa. As we were dancing, I felt deep in my heart a sensation I had not experienced in a long time. I was profoundly attracted to her, and without beating around the bush, I confessed my feelings. Strangely enough, Luisa said she felt the same about me. In the weeks following the party, we met several times in the streets. We were growing progressively fonder of each other.

Luisa came from a large family of four sisters and three brothers. The two elder sisters were already married, and so was the eldest brother, who lived in Montreal, Quebec, Canada.

One day while we were walking together, she told me she was worried about people spreading rumors about us, and that perhaps it would be better for us to become officially engaged. I was immediately overtaken by a strong sense of fear. I tried to make her understand that my future was quite uncertain, without a job and—worse yet—without any idea about what I was going to do. I told her that my state of uncertainty made me feel so insecure that I was in no condition to undertake any new and long term responsibilities.

Her response was that she loved me very much, that my uncertainty and my problems were her uncertainty and her problems, and that if we confronted them together, perhaps it would have been easier and less painful to find the solutions. Upon hearing Luisa's words, I was very moved, so I explained to her my dreams for the future.

I told her how I envisioned my life—about my ideals and the promises I had made to myself regarding my family, adding that only God knew how long it would take to fulfill them, maybe four or five years or even more; and that our engagement was bound to be a very long one. Again, she calmly replied that a long engagement would not bother her, because she was convinced that I was the one with whom she wanted to spend the rest of her life. She shared all my ideals and my dreams, and for those reasons, she could wait a lifetime. The sincerity, spontaneity, and subdued tone in which she spoke could not but touch a deep, sensitive chord in my heart. And so, I said that I would think about it and let her know my answer.

The following days gave rise to more turmoil in my life, as I wavered in my decision. On the one hand I did not want to bear the responsibility of a long engagement, while on the other I feared that should I refuse her request I could lose her for good—something I did not want to happen. After thoroughly debating the question, I decided in favor of becoming engaged. I went to my mother, who in hearing my request told me to talk to my father for his approval.

A few days later while working on the farm, I opened my heart to him. After hearing me out, he looked deep into my eyes. "Son, you are so young to take on such responsibility."

"Father—" I said, but before I could continue to talk, he held up his hand indicating to stop talking, and then he continued.

"If you become engaged, eventually Luisa's family will find a way to pressure you to get married, and without a job, how are you going to support a wife?"

"They are fine people, sincere people," I replied. "They would not do such thing."

He shook his head. "You just don't understand. When you are young, you think everything must be done now, right now. It doesn't."

"Please, Father, try to understand and give me your approval."

He continued shaking his head. "I think you should wait until you are older, until your eyes are opened to the realities of life."

"Father, I know about life."

"You know nothing." He lowered his voice and then spoke more gently. "Son, try to reason and understand, you cannot offer a girl security. Not now. Not yet."

And of course he was right. With a heavy heart, a few days later I met with Luisa. I explained my father's stand to her, adding that I did not know what to do. On the one hand, I told her, she could make me very happy and I didn't want to lose her. On the other, I didn't want to disobey my father. He did have a point, after all—I had nothing yet to offer her in the way of security, and for that reason I would not consider getting married unless I was able to find a satisfactory occupation that would allow us to conduct a reasonably good way of life, and that we could go on just the way we had been.

Chapter 11

Predictably, Luisa replied she was in complete agreement with me. The only problem, she continued, was that a lot of pressure was being applied on her at home, and that if I did not clarify my intentions to her parents, they would no longer allow her to see me.

After a few days of thinking, I resolved to talk to Luisa's mother, since her father was in Germany. Slowly and very clearly, I explained my situation to the woman, my views on the future, and the conditions that were to guide our relationship and the reasons why I could not get engaged.

She replied that she understood my situation, and for her the most important criterion was the love her daughter and I bore each other, and that I was serious and committed, and not the length of the commitment. As far as she was concerned her daughter and I could wait as long as necessary to get officially engaged. Then she told me that under those circumstances, I could continue to see her daughter. Having reached complete agreement, we awaited further developments.

All the above notwithstanding, the situation bothered me enormously, especially in view of the fact that I had disobeyed my father. Hence, I fervently hoped that my commitment would be no cause for ongoing displeasure for my family.

Around the first week of February, 1966, Luisa informed me that her brother had petitioned the Canadian immigration authorities to have his family move to Canada and that in a few months they would depart for Montreal. That news came down like a bolt from the blue, as it meant that Luisa and I would be separated. Furthermore, with a professional diploma in hand, I had already reached the conclusion that the most suitable thing for me to do would be to settle in Italy, where I could eventually pursue my career.

I tried to explain this to Luisa, who had anticipated what I had to say and immediately interrupted me. She was none too happy with the turn of events either, but she was sure that loving me as much as she did, neither distance nor time would make her change her mind about me. At the moment she had no choice but to follow her family, but once I found a job and got settled, and we could get married, she would return immediately, as the one thing she wanted most in life was to be near me.

She suggested that we remain strong and weather our problems—for with faith in our love and God, one day we would be happily married. Those words from her quickly reassured me and calmed my anxiety.

A few days after this conversation, I bought two books on Canada and began reading them. To my surprise, I learned that it was a very young country, with enormous natural resources and in a phase of significant economic development. I learned further that there would be plenty of employment there, as well as good chances for advancement.

While reading those books, I began to strongly feel deep in my heart that Canada was the place that would allow me to fulfill all my dreams and goals.

The more I thought about it, the more I felt I was on the right track.

As the days went by, I resolved to go to Canada, and then, after getting settled, have my parents and brothers join me there. The thought also crossed my mind that if things did not go well in Canada, surely we could move to the United States without too much difficulty, since my Aunt Carmela already lived there.

While considering these possibilities, my mind wandered to my grandfather Paolo and the promise he had my parents make him before dying—that someday we should all move to America. I couldn't help but visualize his joyful expression, full of light and enthusiasm whenever he spoke of the U.S.; how he extolled its enormous size, its great beauty, and the vast possibilities for finding work. He constantly maintained that America had been blessed by God—for it was the land of riches, opportunity, and liberty. When he spoke those words, I was still too young to understand what he was talking about. Now,

Chapter 11

half a century later, I fully understand what his heart was feeling and what he was so fervently trying to explain to us.

All these ideas made my heart overflow with eagerness and excitement. No longer had I any doubts about the proper course to follow—one which would someday make it possible for my family and me to be reunited in one location, living close to one another in harmony, prosperity, and comfort. One day, full of excitement, I spoke about my plans to my father, explaining that Luisa and her family were going to soon move to Montreal. I told him the first thing I should do was to avoid military service, which in my case would have been a simple waste of time. The best way to do this, I explained, was to join my brother in Germany and then transfer to Canada, where I would petition to have the whole family join me.

After I stopped talking, I noticed my father's face had taken up a rather serious expression, manifesting a combination of love, fear, sadness, and perplexity. I asked what was worrying him. He said he was not happy with my plan. I asked why. He answered that for me to be able to immigrate to Canada, I had to get married to Luisa immediately.

I said that was not necessary. Then he asked how I was planning to get my visa. I answered there had to be a way for me to immigrate without having to get married. He felt certain that would not be possible, and even if I managed to get an immigrant visa without getting married, surely upon my reaching Canada, Luisa's family would find a way of inducing me into marriage as soon as possible. According to my father, that would not only abort my future dreams, but also in essence render futile all the family's and my sacrifices in getting a diploma—which in Canada had little, if any, value. Ultimately I would be left with only one alternative—becoming a manual laborer.

After a moment, I calmly explained that I had given the matter a lot of serious thought, and my plan was the one that would make possible the family's future settling in a place where we could work and prosper together. As far as my studies were concerned, I reassured him, they were not fruitless. Sooner or later, I was sure they would help me in any endeavor I chose.

Despite my efforts to be logical, my father shook his head in dissention. He was fully convinced the reason for my desire to go to Canada was my falling in love with Luisa and losing all sense of reason in the process.

Then calmly he looked me straight in the eyes and asked if I truly loved the girl. I replied I did. Next he asked if the girl loved me and if she would eventually be willing to return from Canada and settle in Italy if I were not able to get an immigrant visa. I replied that I had no doubts whatsoever about her love for me, and that if I decided to stay in Italy, she would undoubtedly come back.

Once more, my father shook his head, smiling at the same time as if to indicate his skepticism. His advice was that I get a job in Italy, and then if I were still in love with Luisa, I could marry her, thus avoiding the need to immigrate to another country as Gioacchino had done.

I couldn't help but perceive the real reason he seemed skeptical of my plans: he was afraid to lose me. While I loved Luisa very much, I told him she had in no way influenced my decision to go to Canada. That was an idea that had developed in my own mind—and was influenced by no one on the outside. The only reason I wanted to go to Canada was not to follow my girl, but because I felt deep in my heart that it was the most efficient and practical way for us all to eventually settle down in one place. I was sure that Canada offered what we needed and were looking for.

Enraged at my stubbornness, my father reiterated, *"The brashness of youth blinds you to the truth and the reality of life Paolo."* I assured him I believed in what I said, and for that reason, if for nothing else, he should give me his blessing and permission, so that I could at least attempt to carry out my future plans. I further explained that this was perhaps the best chance I had to discover and fully assess the strength of my character as to whether I had the stuff to accomplish my heart's desire.

I promised that if things did not work out the way I had planned

Chapter 11

I would return to Italy, and together we would find a place where our whole family could settle down as best we could. Mindful of my great determination and relentless persistence, and realizing perhaps that I was right—after all, he too obviously wanted to keep the family together—my father reluctantly gave in. If going to Canada without getting married right away was what I truly wanted, then I was free to follow my aspirations. He also added that I could keep in touch with the young lady, but he would still refuse me permission to get officially engaged because of my age. I hugged and thanked him—assuring him that with God's help our dream one day would become reality.

Paolo During Military Service in Lecce, Italy, 1966.

CHAPTER 12
Travels, Military Service and Engagement

A few days later, I obtained the visa for Germany and immediately informed Gioacchino of my imminent departure. The day before I left, a friend named Salvatore Palumbo asked me what in heaven's name made me want to go abroad instead of finding a job in Italy. As I had done with my father, I explained to him my plans for the future, and like my father, he tried to point out the difficulties that lay ahead and reprimanded me for letting my imagination get out of hand. As I had with my father, I assured him that my goal, while difficult, was within the realm of possibility. I concluded by invoking my favorite motto:

"VOLERE SIGNIFICA POTERE!"
(To Want Means To Be Able To!)

Salvatore smiled and shook his head, as if to say he couldn't believe what he was hearing. He wished me a good journey and good luck. I never forgot this conversation as it reinforced my determination to succeed in my quest.

The following morning I left for Offenburg, Germany. This time, as opposed to the previous trip, I knew what was awaiting me and kept reminding myself of the need to overcome any hardships that might come my way.

Not long after arriving, and with my brother's help, I was able to find a job as a manual laborer, thus beginning a new phase of my life. Memories of that period are still vivid. Until then I had assumed I was very strong-willed and would be able to overcome any obstacles that crossed my path—but was that really true? With the passage of time, the fatigue of manual labor set in, a sensation that made me realize how relatively easy my life had been in Italy. It occurred to me that I had been foolish to persist in this kind of work, and that perhaps my father had been right all along—that I should have followed his advice.

Such reflections were naturally discouraging and caused an incessant psychological struggle within me—casting serious doubts on my capabilities, my ability to achieve my goals, and on what I had believed to be my strength of character. But my brother encouraged me and so did those familiar and powerful words: "***VOLERE SIGNIFICA POTERE!***" *(**To Want Means To Be Able To!**)* I clenched my teeth and stubbornly carried on with my work.

One day, I wrote a letter to Luisa's father, who was also working in Germany, and explained the way I felt about his daughter. I asked his permission to write her. He replied that even if he were satisfied with my intentions, several stumbling blocks worried him very much.

First, he was concerned that I had a professional diploma, whereas his daughter was a simple girl destined to become a plain housewife. The difference in our educational background could in time cause serious problems. Another source of worry was that his family would soon move to Canada and since I was so very young I could meet another girl with an educational background similar to mine who could make me completely forget his daughter, thus causing both him and Luisa great sorrow.

My reply to his letter outlined my plans for the future and vigorously assured him that although I was young and had not yet been called upon to demonstrate the strength of my character, I had full confidence in the strength of my will and the depth of my feelings for his daughter. I added that I would never have written him had I for one moment doubted my ability to bring my promises to an honorable conclusion. Only time, I told him, would demonstrate the truth of my words.

Chapter 12

About a week later I received my reply. Luisa's father explained that even though he understood what I was saying, he still had no guarantee I would keep my promises. Reluctantly, he agreed to allow Luisa and me to write to each other, hoping that in the long run everything would turn out for the best. I knew he was still not confident in me nor was he happy in his decision to allow us to correspond.

Although I was elated, I was also hurt and even bitter about his doubts regarding my intentions. Setting aside my personal feelings, I decided to concentrate on my future, knowing time would prove me right. All I could think about was being able to immigrate to Canada without first having to get married.

About the middle of April 1966, I received a registered letter from my mother, informing me that I had been called to active duty in the Italian armed forces and unless I appeared at the appointed date, I would be declared a deserter. Here was another blow to my future. I didn't know what to do. If I were to join the army, fifteen months of my life would be wasted, but if I didn't, I would be in trouble with the Italian government should I decide to return to Italy. After much reflection and with my brother's advice, I decided in favor of the military.

On my return trip to Sicily, instead of feeling disappointment, I felt a sense of relief that I would no longer have to do manual labor in Germany. This realization seemed like a confirmation to me that I was not strong enough of character to swallow the bitter pill of physical labor. What was happening to me? What would I do when I reached Canada, where my only means of support would be derived from the sweat of my brow? Would my willpower sustain me in achieving my goals?

I arrived in Ribera on the evening of April 18. The next morning I went to the police station and was informed I was being assigned to a school for non-commissioned officers in Lecce.

Later in the town square, I met up with Pippo Sutera, an old schoolmate who had graduated from the technical school the year before I did. Since I had not seen him in a long time, I asked him what

*From the left: Pippo Ferrera, Pina, Franca Sutera,
Ninetta Ferrera, Pippo Sutera and Paolo. Joshua Tree, CA, July, 2004.*

Chapter 12

he was doing. He said he was in the army, and that he was home on a ten-day leave. Then he told me that while in the service, he found out the Canadian government had recently passed a law that granted an immigrant visa to anyone with a degree in agriculture. He had applied and his application was accepted. As soon as he received his visa, he was going to ask the Italian army for a discharge so he could immigrate to Montreal right away.

I could not believe what I was hearing. This was exactly what I had been searching and hoping for. I told him about my own plans, thanked him for the information, and assured him he was a lifesaver. When we parted, we agreed to meet again in Montreal. Two days later, I left for Lecce.

After settling in the army school, I sent an application to the Canadian Embassy in Rome requesting my immigrant visa. Soon thereafter I received confirmation that my application had been accepted, but I would have to wait for paperwork to be completed before a visa could be issued. I began the waiting process.

The first five months of military service turned out to be rather interesting. I learned many new things, and the superiors treated all of us recruits with courtesy—making our homesickness and harsh discipline easier to bear. After five months of training, I was promoted along with everyone in my class to the rank of corporal major and was relocated to the Training Center for Recruits in Nocera Inferiore, Salerno Province, where after five months of duty, I was promoted to sergeant.

Here the atmosphere was quite different from the one in Lecce. The staff couldn't have cared less about what was going on. The barracks were dirty and not the least bit inviting; the food left a lot to be desired; the preparation of our officers was inferior; and they treated us badly. Life in the barracks was monotonous, causing me to lose whatever interest I might have had in doing anything constructive. After a short time I became brazen and impudent like everyone else. On November 15, 1966, I received a letter from Luisa informing me her family had obtained their visas from the Canadian Embassy, and on the twenty-first of the same month, they were going to move to Montreal. As soon as I got this news, I went straight to my superiors to ask for a short leave so I could go home for a visit.

The day after my arrival, I went to help my father in the fields. While we were working, I hesitantly told him that we needed to talk. He asked what was on his mind. I cautiously explained that in a few days Luisa and her family would be moving to Canada and that before they left I wanted to become officially engaged. I asked for his permission and blessing.

He resolutely replied that we had already discussed the subject, and that his mind had not changed. Half exasperated, half conciliatory, I entreated him not to lose his trust in me, as I would see to it someday that he would be proud of having consented to my plea. He repeated his contention that I was too young to get engaged because that would lead me to get married soon after. He was sure that doing so would mess up my life and my future.

I told him I didn't need to get married to get an immigrant visa and told him what I had learned from Pippo Sutera. I left for last the news that I had already applied to the Canadian Embassy and they had already accepted my application.

Whether he was convinced by my pleading or resigned that nothing could make me change my mind, he hugged me. With tears in his eyes, he reminded me how difficult it would be for both him and my mother to see another son depart from home without even knowing when—if ever—they would see me again. In Gioacchino's case, he said, at least they had a chance to see him once a year. But in my case, being so far way, who knew what would happen?

He went on to say that if getting engaged and going to Canada was what I desired and if I truly believed I would be happy with my decision—then so be it. He would give me his permission and blessing to get engaged, and he would go speak to Luisa's parents.

Moved to tears, I managed to stammer a few words of thanks.

Chapter 12

Paolo's passport picture taken in 1967.

CHAPTER 13
Montreal

That evening, my whole family and I went to Luisa's house, where she and her family were waiting for us. Luisa and I became formally engaged. Two days later, as my fiancée and her family were heading for Canada, I went back to my barracks in Nocera Inferiore.

A few weeks later by letter my fiancée informed me that she and her family had adapted very well to life in Canada. They had all found employment and were earning decent wages. She went on to relate that Montreal was a beautiful, modern city with plenty of work available and many opportunities to go into business. While reading her letter, my heart overflowed with joy.

By February 1967, I received a letter from the Canadian Embassy with an appointment for my interview, a medical exam and certification of my school transcripts. After all the examinations, they said everything was in order and they needed my passport. By then, since I was close to completing my term of military service, I decided to get that behind me before applying for my passport.

While I was biding my time waiting for my discharge, I stopped receiving letters from my mother. This was rather strange, as she had been writing me every week. I tried not to worry and blamed my lack of mail on the inefficiency of the postal service, but I was filled with anxiety nonetheless.

Finally, about six weeks later, I received a letter from my brother Ignazio explaining that Mother had been sick, but she was getting better and would soon be writing me herself. Two weeks after that, I received a very short letter from her, assuring me her condition was

Chapter 13

improving and she would be back on her feet very soon.

The news calmed me somewhat, but I still felt troubled. So I asked my superiors for a short leave. They refused me, since in a few weeks my military service would be over. In fact, on the morning of July 20, I was informed I had completed military duty and was free to pack up to go home the following day.

The news was received with such excitement by the entire regiment that we spent the whole night making noise and poking fun at all those in the company who had not yet finished their tour of duty.

Upon arriving back home, I was greeted by a barrage of visiting friends and relatives who declared it a miracle my mother was still alive. After everyone left, my father confided that my mother had been seriously ill since May, and that despite all the medical attention she received in Ribera, she had only gotten worse. Her symptoms were similar to the ones she had experienced in the past: vomiting, headache, and dizziness. One evening, all four of the town's physicians assembled in our house. After a very thorough examination, they came to a general consensus. My mother's condition was so critical that in all probability she wouldn't make it until the next day. They advised my father to be strong.

My father asked the doctors if they knew of any specialized clinic in Palermo where he could take her in the hope, however slight, that she could be helped. One of the doctors told him of a specialist and promptly wrote down his name and address.

As some of my aunts and neighbors were getting my mother dressed, my father called upon his godson, Calogero Triolo, to hire a car to take him and my mother to Palermo. Fifteen minutes later, as my father was getting my mother into the car, one of the doctors remarked that she was in no condition to undertake the long trip, predicting she would die before reaching the town of Burgio thirteen miles away.

Looking straight into the doctor's eyes, my father replied that when my mother was no longer breathing and he was certain she was dead, then—and only then—would he tell the driver to return to Ribera. Thus they left for Palermo.

All through the trip, my father watched my mother closely, making sure she was still breathing. When they arrived at the clinic, she was admitted into intensive care and given drugs. As the days went by, she got progressively better. A few weeks later, she was completely cured. "Had I accepted the local doctor's advice," my father concluded, "by now your mother would surely have died."

Deep in my heart, I felt that my father's enormous faith, hope, and determination—aided by a good specialist—were instrumental in saving my mother's life.

Suddenly I realized why I had been so nervous and worried while I was in the army and not receiving news from home. It was likely that I perceived the gravity of my mother's illness. If that were truly the case, how was such a phenomenon possible?

I recalled the first time my mother was ill. The old healer in Marsala blamed her illness on a spell that had been cast by three malevolent women. On that occasion medicine had no effect on her whatsoever, while this time it did.

Here was my dilemma:
- **How was it possible that the first time she was ill the medicine had no effect on my mother, while this time medicine saved her life?**
- Since the symptoms were the same on both occasions, where did they originate?
- Was there a spell?
- What other mysterious causes may have been responsible?
- What was the truth?

Many years were to go by before I could grasp how everything had happened and the precise mechanism that had made it possible.

As soon as I arrived in Ribera, I applied for my passport. But since my mother's illness had eaten away the family savings, I was uncertain

Chapter 13

where the money would come from for me to travel to Canada. I discussed the matter with my father, who told me not to worry, that he would do his best to get a loan.

One evening while sitting at a café in the town square with Enzo Tortorici, he asked how I planned to pay for my trip to Canada. When I replied that my father was trying to negotiate a loan, he expressed how sorry he was that neither he nor his family could offer help. His family's financial condition was no better than mine. I told him not to worry, since I well understood the situation. Then he suggested I might write to Luisa's family and ask them for a loan. I dismissed that notion as humiliating, but he said that since they already knew about my mother's illness, there was nothing degrading in asking them for a favor.

After reflecting on the matter, I reluctantly decided to take Enzo's advice. I wrote to Luisa's parents explaining that I needed a loan to cover the cost of an airplane ticket to Montreal and a few other minor expenses. I assured them I would repay them as soon as I got a job in Canada. I assumed I would hear back within ten days or so, but three weeks went by without a reply—either from my fiancée or from her family. It worried me.

Every evening, as soon as he returned from work, Enzo came by my house and inquired if I had any news from Canada. After a while, he was able to predict my reply by the expression on my face.

One evening as Enzo and I were walking up and down the square, we encountered his father, who asked about news from Canada. Enzo told him I had heard nothing. He reflected a moment and said he would try to secure a loan for me.

Two days later, having received my passport, I was waiting in the square for the bus that would take me to Palermo. From there, I would proceed to Rome and the Canadian Embassy, where my immigration visa would be waiting for me. Seemingly out of nowhere, Enzo's father pulled up on his motorcycle and called me aside. He extracted a bundle of bills from his pockets, one hundred thousand lire, and gave them to me—the equivalent of about two hundred dollars. Apologizing for not being able to do better for me, he said this was all he could borrow. I was astonished and extremely touched by this extraordinary show of affection and asked him if he would please pass by my house and leave the money with my mother. We waved our good-byes, and I boarded the bus.

Upon my return from Rome, my mother informed me that Gioacchino had sent 50,000 lire from Germany, or approximately $100, and that my father was trying to borrow more, hoping to secure sufficient funds to cover my trip expenses.

While waiting for more developments, Enzo convinced me to ask Giuseppe Zabbara's father, our friend who was working in Germany, to lend me the additional money I needed.

When we arrived, Mr. Zabbara asked me if I had set my departure date. I replied in the negative, explaining the reasons why my plans had been thwarted. Looking at me with fatherly affection and without saying anything, he went into another room. A few moments later he came back holding a signed check in hand. As he gave it to me, he asked me to write in the amount I needed and then go to the bank and cash it.

Mr. Zabbara's son Nino, Giuseppe's younger brother, happened to be home. Nino was working as an apprentice in a tailor's shop and told me he was making a brand new suit for me as a departure gift.

All this effusion of trust, friendship, esteem, and love touched me so deeply that I began to cry. I embraced them all and thanked them from the bottom of my heart, saying I was sure I would never again find such good friends as they had been. Mr. Zabbara brushed aside my "childish" expressions of gratitude. He promised that since he was soon going hunting for rabbits, should he be lucky enough to shoot one, he would organize a farewell dinner.

Later that day, I went to purchase an airline ticket and fixed my departure date. The following day a close friend of Luisa's family came to see me. She said she had received a letter from Luisa's parents

Chapter 13

containing a check for fifty dollars and an airplane ticket with instructions to forward it to me. I thanked the woman and took the envelope containing the plane ticket and the check.

It was gratifying to know I had not been forgotten in Canada, but the family's use of an intermediary humiliated me. My family's financial condition had been the subject of discussion outside the family circle. This kind of behavior on the part of Luisa's family left me sad and confused.

I now found myself with two tickets in my possession. I chose to keep the ticket sent by Luisa's parents and got a refund for the one I had purchased earlier, thus giving me a reserve of cash on hand should I not find immediate employment in Canada.

It is hard to express the emotions that pervaded my mind and my heart in those days—hope, joy, sadness, and fear. After two long years of planning and waiting, I was about to begin my journey across the Atlantic Ocean with the hope of fulfilling my dreams for a bright future.

On the morning of September 3, 1967, accompanied by Enzo, Aunt Lina, my parents, and Ignazio, I left for Palermo Airport, where after an emotional goodbye, I took the plane to Rome and subsequently the one to Montreal. At the Montreal airport, Luisa, her family, and some recently emigrated friends of mine—including Pippo Sutera—awaited me with smiling faces.

Paolo at the 1967 Montreal Expo.
The structure behind is the American Pavilion at the Expo 1967, where Paolo got his first job as a janitor in Montreal.

CHAPTER 14
From Joy to Disillusionment

When the plane landed at Montreal Airport, I was excited and, like the other passengers, anxious to get off. Finally, after having encountered so many problems, I was on Canadian soil, ready to begin a new life. In a matter of a few hours, my emotional state had completely shifted—from the grief of parting with my family to the joy of embracing Luisa after such a long separation. As I waited in line for my turn to get through customs, I caught sight of her jumping up and down, handkerchief in hand, shaking her arm vigorously to attract my attention. Instinctively, I mirrored her actions. Those few minutes of delay felt more like hours. When I finally got out of customs, I literally ran to hug her.

"I can hardly believe it," I said breathlessly, my heart pumping wildly. "My dream has finally come true."

"Mine, too," Luisa said, "I can hardly believe you're actually here."

After greeting Luisa's family and all my friends, we proceeded to Luisa's brother's car, which was parked close by. At that point, I couldn't help noticing the local cars were much bigger than those in Italy. Indeed, they looked enormous. As we drove to the family home, I was thoroughly impressed by the wide, clean streets and the sweeping beauty of the city.

"It feels like somewhere in Europe," I said.

"Europe is our past," Luisa said, her arm linked in mine. "This is Canada—our future."

When we reached the family home, I was surprised by the number of Luisa's relatives and my own friends from back in

Ribera that had come to welcome me.

After spending a few minutes with each of them, I called Luisa aside. "I have two cousins living here in Montreal that I would like to locate—Maria and Francesca. They're daughters of my father's sister, my Aunt Giuseppa. Do you think you can help me?"

It was easy enough to find Maria in the phone directory. She was excited to hear of my arrival and asked for my address, promising to call Francesca right away so they could come over and see me. Within an hour, they were there with their families, adding even more joy to what already had been an extraordinary day.

While the party was still going on, I asked Luisa if it were possible to find Aunt Carmela's phone number as well, even though she lived in Waterbury, Connecticut—in the United States. With the help of a friend who spoke English, they dialed information, and in less than five minutes, I had my aunt's telephone number, which I dialed.

When Aunt Carmela answered the phone, and I told her who was calling, she thought someone else was teasing her.

"Aunt Carmela, it's really me—Paolo," I assured her.

Realizing it was no joke, Aunt Carmela screamed with joy and called for her husband, Salvatore, who had no idea what was going on. As we talked, she explained that Montreal was about 350 miles from Waterbury, approximately a six-hour drive. She and Uncle Salvatore would come to see me the following weekend. This was truly incredible news; at long last I would be meeting my Aunt Carmela.

That evening, after all the guests left, I sat at the kitchen table with Luisa and her parents. I asked if they knew where I might find a room to rent. Her father told me I would be welcome to stay and live with them. After reflecting briefly, I replied that if it would not be a burden on them—and if it were truly their wish that I do so—I would gladly accept their offer. "But only until I get settled and I have enough money to rent a small apartment." They all agreed it was a wonderful idea.

"Life in Montreal is different from the one you were used to in

Chapter 14

Ribera," Luisa's father said. "There are so many qualified people here with a diploma or even a university degree that have a hard time getting started in their profession."

I immediately caught the drift and assured him I knew what to expect and was ready to take any available job.

A collective sigh of relief and signs of enthusiasm and optimism broke out over their faces. Luisa's father added that a relative of theirs would pick me up in the morning and take me to the employment office of a cleaning firm that was hiring workers.

The conversation came to an end on that promising note. I thanked them for everything they had done for me—making me feel at ease and welcoming me as one of their own. Then I turned to Luisa's parents, thanked them for the plane ticket and asked how much I owed them.

"Nothing," they replied. Carlo, their eldest son, had financed the ticket through the bank. They suggested I keep the cash and make the monthly payments to the bank.

This kind of bank loan was good news to me, so I smiled appreciatively and accepted their advice. "Thank you also for the check," I said. I took the fifty-dollar check from my wallet and handed it to Luisa's father.

His eyes opened wide in surprise and he drew back. "Oh, no," he said. "That was a gift."

"I asked for a loan, not a gift." I smiled. "And as much as I appreciate your help, I'm duty-bound to return this to you." Then, as cautiously and discreetly as possible, I asked why they had chosen to send the money and the plane ticket to me through their friend instead of directly to me. "One's dirty linen should not be washed in public," I said. "There was no compelling reason to make public my family's precarious financial situation."

Understanding I did not appreciate the way they had handled the matter, they accepted the check silently and turned the conversation to other matters.

After we had all retired to bed, a knock sounded on my door. It was nearly one a.m. Luisa had come to wish me "goodnight." I went to sleep that night feeling I was the luckiest and happiest man on earth.

The following morning, Luisa's cousin accompanied me to the cleaning firm, where he knew the employment clerk. After completing the necessary form, I was offered a job at two dollars an hour. I accepted gladly, and began working the following day at the American Pavilion of the 1967 Montreal International Exposition.

During the first week at the Exposition, I earned ninety-five dollars—more than I had earned in a month as sergeant in the Italian army. I was already beginning to appreciate that Montreal offered excellent opportunities for going into business and making good money—a fact that naturally delighted me and boosted my enthusiasm for the future.

On Friday evening of the same week, Aunt Carmela telephoned from Waterbury informing me she and my uncle were leaving for Montreal on the following morning. They arrived around two o'clock Saturday, and as I embraced them, I felt indescribable joy. I wished Grandfather Paolo and my mother were around to witness this long-awaited moment.

During their stay in Montreal, I outlined my projects for the future, explaining that my primary goal was to get all our family together. This made Aunt Carmela particular happy, since she envisioned the possibility in the not-too-distant future of seeing the sister she had never known. Over the course of the visit, we took many photographs, which I developed and then enclosed in two very long letters—one to my parents and one to Gioacchino—to keep them informed and to suggest it was time for them to get ready the necessary papers for their immigration to Canada. Unfortunately, I counted my chickens before they hatched.

One evening approximately three weeks after my arrival in Montreal, while we were still sitting around the dining table, I asked Luisa's parents how much I owed them for my room and board, and how I might go about sending some money to my parents. They replied that

Chapter 14

I owed them nothing, that they were just happy to help me out.

I tried to make them understand that had I not been working I could see their point, but since I was employed and earning decent money, it wasn't right that I take advantage of their generosity. I told them I appreciated immensely all they had done for me and that they treated me as one of their own children. Once more they told me not to worry about it.

At that point, Maria, one of Luisa's sisters, spoke. "Perhaps the best thing you could do with your money is not pay my parents nor send money to your own—but to save it so you and Luisa can get married."

Just as I was about to address Maria's unexpected comment, her mother told her to be quiet. Speaking very slowly and deliberately, she said, "The long engagement we had originally agreed to in Ribera is no longer feasible here in Montreal. Perhaps you should seriously consider getting married as soon as possible. Once you are married, you'll be able to count on not only your own pay check, but on Luisa's as well. Then you could send money to your parents or allocate it however you wish."

Astonished, I asked why the long engagement was not possible in Montreal. But I received no reply.

Deep in my heart I felt a mixture of fear and rage that made me nervous. When I calmed, I said, "While I am grateful to you for all you have done for me, I do not believe you have the right to tell me what to do and how and when to do it. My family means everything to me, and I would never allow anyone under any circumstances to come between us."

From the silence that followed, and the stone-faced expressions staring back at me, I knew I had caught them off-guard—just as they had caught me. I continued to tell them I had left Italy for three reasons:

- **To reunite my family**
- **To give myself and my family a chance to improve our way of life.**

- **To be close to their daughter**

"Taking on the responsibilities of married life would become a stumbling block to building a stable future," I said. "Without a valid job, there is nothing I can offer your daughter except insecurity and the low wages of a manual laborer."

Getting no reaction, I continued, "There is no way for me to find a better job in Montreal unless I can speak English or French—and if I am working eight to ten hours a day, there's little time to learn a new language."

They were not paying attention, so I raised my voice. "Before leaving Ribera, I made certain promises that I still intend to keep. Of course, there is no guarantee I will succeed, but I will have peace of mind only if I try as hard as I can. Frankly," I said, "I do not feel I'm mature enough at this time to take on the responsibility of marriage."

No one spoke. "Please try to understand," I said, "I love Luisa, and I want to provide her with a stable future and a good life, which I would not be able to do if I rushed to get married. It's just not time yet."

My candor was met with gloom-and-doom glances. No one uttered a word.

Luisa's eyes filled with tears. I motioned to her to follow me outside, where I asked her why she was crying. As she blotted her tears, she said she was afraid our engagement would come to an end.

I assured her our love was bigger than those issues, and in the end her parents would come to see I was right and would agree to abide by our original plan. "I hope so." Luisa pressed her head to mine.

Two days later I finished work earlier than normal and got home before Luisa. I thought it would be nice to pick her up from work and accompany her back home, so I asked her mother for the address of the factory where Luisa worked. She declined to give me the information, explaining that people would gossip if they saw us alone together on the bus. Unprepared for that kind of response, I felt hurt, considering

Chapter 14

all I had endured to get my own parents' approval of the engagement.

I responded bitterly to her insinuations. I reminded her that in Ribera, before Luisa and I were engaged, it never bothered her that people would gossip about us by seeing us unescorted in public. Now that we were officially engaged and I had travelled halfway around the world, I had earned the right to be with Luisa. She had no reason to worry about gossip.

I didn't buy that things were "different" in Montreal, and for that reason, I didn't hesitate to tell her she should be more concerned about what I was thinking than anyone else.

My comments threw her into a frenzy, and she rushed to her bedroom and locked herself inside. Once alone, I regretted what I had said, even though I was still convinced I was right. I wondered how it was possible that in such a short span of time, everything that had seemed so wonderful had collapsed into such a woeful mess.

That afternoon, when Luisa returned from work, I told her what had happened between her mother and me. Under the circumstances, I thought it would be best to look for my own apartment. Luisa dissolved into tears. Her reaction shocked me. I had expected her support and the reassurance that everything would be all right—that she would intervene with her mother and iron things out. I wondered what had happened to the fortitude and determination she had shown at the beginning of our relationship.

The following Wednesday was my day off. Around six that morning, I heard on the radio that the bus drivers' union had been unable to reach an agreement with the City of Montreal and was going on strike. This was bad news for those of us who relied on public transportation to commute to work. Some people who lived close to their jobs were able to walk, but most of us had to rely on a taxi or other means of transportation. Luisa's factory was a distance from home, and she could not find a cab that morning. Without hesitation, her mother called the woman who lived in the apartment above us and who also happened to be from Ribera. She asked if her son, who had a car, would be able to drive Luisa.

The woman got her son out of bed, and ten minutes later he was at the door. I was furious. There I was, engaged to Luisa, and yet could not be trusted to know where she worked. Yet, here was this other young man—practically a stranger—driving her there. I couldn't help but wonder if the boy and his family—already aware of the problems I had been having with my fiancée's parents—wouldn't be laughing their heads off at this irony. What bothered me most was that Luisa accepted it passively—and without concern for my feelings.

When I confronted Luisa's mother later on, politely trying to explain that what she had done was out of line and inconsiderate towards me, she became furious and accused me of jealousy.

"This is not about jealousy—it's about respect for your daughter's fiancé," I said.

Luisa's mother struggled to breathe, and I began to panic. If anything were to happen to her, I would end up blaming myself.

That afternoon, Carlo, Luisa's eldest brother, returned from work earlier than usual. Unaware of what had transpired that morning, he asked me to accompany him to pick up his sister from work.

"Sorry, Carlo," I said sarcastically. "If I were to learn the location of Luisa's work and if we were to ever break our engagement, Luisa would be permanently dishonored, and she would never be able to find a husband."

He saw there was a problem and suggested I come along with him so we could talk about it. I took this as a chance to confide in a member of the family who might be interested in my side of the story. On the way to the factory, I filled Carlo in on everything that had taken place over the past days between his mother and me.

He seemed sorry for what I had been going through and assured me he understood my position. He promised to work things out with his mother when we got back home. After we picked up Luisa and made it back home, we found everyone at the house in a miserable mood, so nothing was said at that point.

Chapter 14

Following supper, Luisa's father called me aside to speak with me. We withdrew to the foyer, where he shut the door behind us to ensure our privacy.

"I'm sorry to have to tell you this, Paolo, but the long engagement we agreed upon in Ribera is no longer possible. My wife and I are not well, and for that reason we want to get our family settled as soon as possible so the two of us can return to Ribera."

Now I knew the real reason they were in such a hurry to marry off their daughter. I assured him I was sorry about their problems, but that I too had problems and responsibilities to cope with—and could not agree to these new terms. Then, feeling exasperated, I looked him straight in the eye and asked him, "Do you recall when we were both in Germany, and I sent you a letter asking permission to write to Luisa?"

He nodded.

"And do you recall being worried that I was too young and immature and might forget Luisa over time, causing you, your daughter, and your family considerable grief in the process?"

Again, he nodded.

"And yet," I said, "as young and immature as you thought I was, I have kept my promise. You, the older and supposedly the wiser and more mature one, have forsaken yours. It is not right that you neglected to tell me about all this at the outset, right after you arrived in Montreal, and allow me a chance to decide on my own what to do—instead of letting me endure all the hardships and expenses I incurred by immigrating. If you think you or your family can manipulate me, you are wrong, sir. I will decide when I am ready to marry, and no one else."

He sat there in shock as I continued. "Furthermore, if my parents—whom I love dearly and who have given me everything they could until a few weeks before I left Italy—if they were unable to change my mind about my engagement to your daughter, then imagine how you, whom I barely know, could even dream of influencing my course of action."

Shame and humiliation was evident on his face. No doubt, he had not expected me to be so bold in expressing my feelings.

With his voice barely audible and eyes pointed to the ground, he admitted I was right and was very sorry if in some way or other he and his family had created problems for me. "Nevertheless," he insisted, "for the very reasons I have just outlined, a long engagement in Montreal would be impossible. I advise you to take this matter seriously."

I understood that in a discreet and diplomatic way, without saying it, he was telling me if I would not agree to get married as soon as possible, the engagement would be broken.

In that moment I recalled the words my father once uttered to me:

"The brashness of youth blinds you to the truth and the reality of life Paolo."

How true were those words, and how wise had been his counsel!

What a pity we wait until we are older to appreciate the wisdom our parents pass along to us when we are young!

Since neither of us had anything more to add, we both went quietly inside the house, where the whole family was seated, looking concerned. Luisa sobbed silently. I was nervous, fearful, and angry, but resolute. Regardless of the consequences, I was determined not to cave in to their wishes.

We went on like that until Saturday of the same week, my day off. While I was still in bed, I overheard Luisa's mother talking on the phone. I gathered that a cousin of mine—the son of my father's eldest sister—had come to Montreal from Elizabeth, New Jersey, and was staying with friends. During that whole conversation, she never said anything to my cousin about my living in her house, nor did she say anything to me afterward. That was the final warning signal—I could no longer stay in that house. I got up and began packing my suitcase.

Liborio Zambito and Paolo.
Montreal, October 1967.

CHAPTER 15
Dark and Challenging Days

But where could I go? I called Liborio Zambito, a friend of mine from Ribera. He was a butcher, alone in Montreal and boarding with an old Italian couple. I explained my predicament, and asked him if he knew of a room for rent. He told me he did not, but if we wanted and if his landlord would allow it, I could share his small room with him. I answered yes. After approximately five minutes, he phoned me back, telling me that I could move in any time I wanted for thirty-five dollars a week, the same amount he was paying. I thanked him for his help and called a taxi.

As the car pulled up, Luisa went to her room to cry. Overcome with emotion and with tears in my eyes, I shook hands with those members of the family who were present. When I reached Luisa's mother, I asked her if she could still respect the terms of the original engagement agreement. She replied that it was impossible. I said the engagement was over and she was free to give her daughter's hand in marriage to whomever she pleased. Then, I took my suitcases and left.

Once again I had experienced misfortune. In just a few days all the dreams I had held dear for two long years had vanished into thin air. I could hardly fathom how over forty days I had fallen from the greatest peaks of joy to the lowest levels of disillusionment. The anguish was simply too strong to bear, so I went to a liquor store and bought a bottle of whiskey to drown my sorrows.

Just as I made it home, Liborio was getting back from work. When he saw me with a liquor bottle in my hand, he realized what I had in mind and grabbed it away, assuring me it was the wrong thing to do. I knew he was right, and let it go. I would never allow myself to be that weak again.

My cousins Francesca and Maria with their families and my friends Liborio Zambito, Pippo Sutera, Vincenzo D'Anna and Emanuele Territo helped me immensely in getting through that dark period of my life. Everybody treated me like a brother, especially my cousins, who constantly invited me to their homes to get my mind off my problems. I never forgot their kindness, their love and their support.

From the left: Cousin Maria, Paolo, Cousin Francesca. Montreal, 1990.

A few days after recuperating from the shock of my broken engagement, I wrote Gioacchino and my parents, informing them. I assured them I was all right—I was keeping up with my work in the hope of carrying out our future plans.

My mother sent back a long letter asking me to return at once to Ribera and not to worry about the expense because they would help me out. I replied that Montreal was a beautiful city and in time perhaps it could offer us the bright future we were all seeking. I asked that she and my father stop worrying about me and stay on track so we could accomplish our common goal—to bring the whole family together.

Gioacchino wrote that since I was determined to stay in Canada, he would go to the Canadian embassy in Germany for an immigrant visa and join me in Montreal as soon as possible.

In the meantime, I sent all the money I could save to my parents to pay the debts I had incurred before leaving Italy. On October 25, 1967, six months after it opened, the Montreal Exposition closed down—along with my job. With the winter approaching, I was worried about getting more work. Fortunately, with the help of an old friend and neighbor from Ribera, Domenico Bavetta, I was able to find a position in a men's clothing factory. The pay was only one dollar and ten cents an hour. Working over fifty hours a week, I was able to bring home about forty-five dollars. I was paying thirty-five dollars for room and board, so I was left with a grand total of approximately ten dollars a week to cover my bus fare and miscellaneous expenses. I spent a lot of time analyzing the obstacles that stood in the way of achieving my goals.

My immediate challenges were to:
- **Learn one of the official languages of Canada: French or English.**
- **Discover the kind of work I liked so in time I could pursue a business of my own.**
- **Devise a system for saving money for starting the business.**

Now, all of this seemed easy enough to think and talk about, but where was I supposed to begin? Learning a foreign language without going to school was a difficult and slow process, especially living as I did among other immigrants who had little command of French or English. And then, how could I learn a new trade without knowing what I really wanted to do? Finally, how could I save any money with only ten dollars left over each week for miscellaneous expenses? I was losing my willpower and doubting that my goals would ever be fulfilled. During those frequent moments of weakness, I tried to recall as often as I could the old saying that had always helped me in the past:

"VOLERE, SIGNIFICA POTERE!"
(To Want Means To Be Able To!)

With that powerful message in mind, I went on grinding my teeth and carrying on with my everyday existence as well as I could.

By this time, word had spread in Ribera about the breakup of my engagement. I received lots of letters from friends and relatives encouraging me to keep my chin up. A friend of mine named Giuseppe Miceli, who lived in the nearby town of Cattolica Eraclea, wrote a beautiful letter encouraging me not to worry, adding that in time everything was bound to work for the best. He went on to ask what I was doing and what I planned for the future.

After reflecting a while about what I would say, I started writing—thanking him for his letter and for our deep and sincere friendship. I went on to explain that I felt "as if I were in a dark, seemingly interminable tunnel, at the end of which I could barely discern a glimmer of light." The tunnel represented my present life, and the glimmer of light symbolized my future and my goals in life. I wrote that "if I keep walking without giving in to fatigue or to the many obstacles one encounters when walking in darkness—

and at this moment I am certainly in the greatest darkness I can imagine—then, sooner or later, I will reach the end of the tunnel, breathe fresh air, and reach the daylight."

I was trying to convey to my friend that in Montreal there were enormous opportunities, but I wasn't ready to take advantage of them, since I still didn't have the necessary knowledge, preparation and experience to properly exploit them. Therefore, I was forced into serving a long apprenticeship, which, if effectively completed, would ultimately allow me to reap the benefits of my sacrifices.

One evening around the middle of December, I returned from work and found a letter in the mailbox from Giannina, the girl I had considered my first love. It was a beautiful, friendly letter, full of encouraging advice. She invited me to write and tell her how I was getting along. After reading her letter, I felt uplifted. I answered immediately, thanking her for her kind thoughts. And so we began to write back and forth. From her letters I could easily understand, even if she didn't say so openly, that she was very fond of me. Searching deep in my heart, I couldn't help thinking that notwithstanding all I had been through in the past few years, I was still very fond of her. Just the thought of her lifted the daily burden of sorrow I carried.

Another evening, after returning from work, I found one of Giannina's letters. She wanted to know when I was going back to Ribera, as she wanted very much to see me. Now I had no more doubts. She really was in love with me, but was not telling me openly, hoping I would take the first step. After analyzing my feelings, I convinced myself that despite the passage of time I had never stopped loving her. This complicated even more my already complex situation. Listening to the voice of my heart, I wanted to say how much I loved her, that I had never stopped loving her, and that I would take the first flight available in order to hold her in my arms. But where would I find the money to undertake such a trip? And even if I could get a loan to return to Sicily, what would I be able to tell her once I got there? That I would settle down in Italy? Wouldn't that mean abandoning all my plans for the future?

Now, if I could convince Giannina to come back to Montreal with me—what sort of future could I offer her? The idea of explaining the whole situation to her flashed through my mind many times over.

The questions were:
- **Would she understand my situation?**
- **Could I ask her to wait for me without knowing how long it would take to realize my plans?**
- **How long would she be willing to wait?**

Once again, I was very confused, demoralized, and filled with fear. I was afraid to make promises I might not be able to keep. Above all, I feared losing her once again.

After thinking long and hard on the right course of action, I finally decided this was not the time to consider restarting a love relationship with Giannina—our bond had perhaps ended before it began a few years earlier, and it would be terribly difficult to turn back the clock—even at the painful cost of losing her.

Reluctantly and sadly I wrote her a letter, knowing instinctively it would be my last one. I told her I was very happy in Montreal and earning plenty of money. I added that Canadian girls enjoyed a great deal of freedom, making it possible for young men to date them on weekends. I went on to say how much fun I was having—going dancing and all. "Why would I want to change such a pleasant state of affairs by going back to Ribera?" I asked her.

I couldn't help but cry while committing those words to paper. For the first time in my life, I had done the thing I detested the most—I had lied. I was not only lying to another human being, but I was lying to myself about my true feelings. I knew this letter would put an end to a relationship that had been my only source of joy during that bleak period of my life. I decided it would be best to suffer in silence and let my life follow its natural chaotic course rather than expose her to the truth of my miserable condition.

I sealed the letter, affixed a stamp, and said, "Goodbye." Just as I had imagined, Giannina never replied. That chapter of my life would now be closed forever.

CHAPTER 16
I Meet the Girl of My Dreams
My Family Comes to America
Gioacchino & I Move to Waterbury Connecticut

In January of 1968, I received a letter from a Quebec government office inviting me to enroll in a ten-week course in French. Not only was the course free, but students were also to receive thirty-five dollars a week. I immediately thought of accepting the offer, but on further consideration, I realized I didn't have a penny in the bank. Since I was paying thirty-five dollars a week for my room and board, where would I find the money for bus fare and other small expenses? I spoke about this to my cousins. Maria and her husband told me not to worry. I could live with them for twenty dollars a week while I was taking the course. I immediately accepted their generous offer. On the following day I enrolled in the course, fully convinced that with literacy in French, I would be able to find a better paying job.

The first day of class was marvelous—reminding me of my old school days in Sicily. Here, however, there were students from practically every country of the world. My attention was diverted in particular by two young women who struck me as being from Italy. During our break, noticing they both wore graduation rings like my own, I gathered the courage to approach them and ask if they were Italian.

"Yes," came the answer with a smile.

"Are you Sicilian?" I asked, this time in Italian.

"Yes." The reply was in Italian.

With a broadening grin, I leaned closer. "Are you from Agrigento Province?"

Pina in Montreal, 1968.

Chapter 16

"Yes!" Their look of surprise matched my own.

"Do you have diplomas from high school or university?"

Looking at me with a slight smile that seemed to express a combination of curiosity and suspicion, the one I thought to be the younger of the two spoke. "How do you know so much about us?" she asked.

Her facial expression, her smile, and the grace of her movements delighted me. In the seconds that followed, while trying to formulate the answer to her question, deep in my heart I felt that she was the girl I had to marry at any cost. She would be my perfect match, my ideal lifelong companion. I smiled and pointed to her ring finger. "I have one just like it. I'm from Ribera and I have a diploma from the technical school of Sciacca."

"We're practically neighbors!" they answered in unison. "We're from Cattolica Eraclea."

I was familiar with that small town only eighteen kilometers from my Ribera.

The younger woman said she had spent her last school year in Ribera attending Il Magistrale, the local teacher's school, and her sister had a teacher's diploma as well. They had come to Montreal in the hope of finding work and prosperity.

We introduced ourselves, and I learned they were Paola and Pina. Pina was the younger of the two—the one I felt I had to marry.

As the days went by, I became increasingly aware of just how attractive, charming, intelligent, and serious they were—and that Pina had all the prerequisites for being the excellent wife and the source of happiness for which I had long searched—so far, in vain. My attraction towards Pina continued to grow until I was tempted to confess my love. But by then I was so afraid of suffering another terrible disappointment, I held onto my instincts, which told me to wait for the right moment. In the interim, I kept quiet and never socialized—either with Pina or anyone else.

In February of 1968, Sicily was hit by a series of earthquakes that practically destroyed the towns of Gibellina and Santa Margherita—the epicenter of the quake. Many people lost their lives. Although not as badly hit, nearby towns suffered significant damage. Luckily, the walls of our house showed only a few cracks—nothing when compared to the damages suffered by so many other families.

On April 10, my French class came to an end, and I was able to speak, read, and write in French with a certain amount of ease. The realization, of course, made me feel more secure.

My brother Gioacchino wrote from Germany. He said the Canadian Embassy had granted him an immigrant visa and that he would arrive in Montreal around mid-April. That bit of news made me ecstatic, since the first significant step had now been taken in bringing the family together.

Gioacchino came to live with me at the home of our cousin Maria. Later, we rented a small apartment, which we were supposed to move into by May 1.

The close of the Exposition had sent Montreal into a recession. Jobs were difficult to find, particularly in construction, which was the field in which Gioacchino and I wanted to work.

In the meantime, Francesca's eldest son, who was close to my age, had decided to go to Winnipeg, in the province of Manitoba, where work was supposedly plentiful.

After consulting with Gioacchino, I thought it wise to go there with him and try my luck—with the expectation that Gioacchino would come as soon as my cousin and I found work.

Before I left for Winnipeg, I debated if I should disclose my feelings to Pina. But because of the customs of the day, that would mean getting engaged, and feeling I wasn't ready for that, I decided to wait. Deep inside my heart I felt everything was going to be okay and I was not going to lose her.

Upon reaching Winnipeg, my cousin, who was an electrician, immediately found a job with Hydro Manitoba whereas I, having no

Chapter 16

trade upon which to rely, was forced to work as a gardener at an hourly wage of one dollar-seventy-five. Nonetheless, I was filled with renewed hope and enthusiasm.

We spent our first Saturday night in Winnipeg going dancing. By chance we happened to meet two young men, also immigrants from Agrigento Province, and specifically from a town called Aragona. As soon as we found out we were from the same province, we talked and soon became good pals. One of them, Leonardo Cacciatore, told us he had been living in Winnipeg for over a year and liked it very much. He said he worked in a sheet metal factory, where he earned a good salary. During those initial days in Winnipeg, Leonardo was of great help. His friendship—and the fact that Winnipeg was a nice city with plenty of job opportunities—elevated my hopes.

I wrote Gioacchino and told him I would send him the first money I earned so he could join me as soon as possible. I asked him to tell the landlord in Montreal that because of work, we had to move to Winnipeg and could no longer pay rent on his apartment. This, of course, was more easily said than done. The landlord threatened that if we didn't fulfill the terms of the rental contract, he would take us to court. This new development sent all our plans into limbo, as I had no way of knowing how the legal consequences of such an action would affect our Canadian residency status. I felt compelled to return to Montreal, hoping to go back to Winnipeg the following year.

In Montreal, I found work in a paint factory, where the hourly wage was one dollar-fifty. Gioacchino had already found work in a textile company at one dollar twenty-five, so we managed to survive. It was during this time that we became friends with Rocco, Gioacchino's coworker, who was from Cattolica Eraclea.

In post-earthquake Sicily, things had begun to calm down, despite the fact that thousands remained homeless and without families. The U.S. government, moved by the plight of displaced people, passed an emergency law allowing those families with relatives in the United States and whose homes had been damaged or destroyed in the earthquake to immigrate to America if they were able to get an affidavit of support from their U.S.-based relatives. As so often happens in life, the tragedy of some often brings about the good fortune of others. That was the case with us and many other families who were able to enter the United States as a result of the devastating natural disaster.

Approximately twelve years earlier, my family had sent applications for immigration to the U.S. Now, with their home damaged by the earthquake, they finally qualified for admission—and within a few months received their visas. On September 9, 1968, exactly one year and six days after my own departure, and about six months after that of Gioacchino, my father, mother, and brother Ignazio took a flight from Palermo, arriving several hours later at J.F.K International Airport in New York. Gioacchino and I took a bus from Montreal and were there at the airport to meet them. Also awaiting their arrival were Aunt Carmela and Uncle Salvatore, as well as my Aunt Lina—Grandmother Antonina's sister—and her children.

It was wonderful to hug my parents and brother Ignazio once again. But the most moving, emotionally-charged moment of that day occurred when my mother and her sister—Aunt Carmela—saw each other for the first time. It was almost unbelievable—after forty-five years my mother was finally able to embrace her sister. It was a moment to remember all the rest of our lives.

Later, we went to Aunt Carmela's house in Waterbury—about 120 miles from the airport. Awaiting us there was a multitude of relatives we were meeting for the first time, as well as many friends of my aunt and uncle.

Aunt Carmela and Uncle Salvatore had already rented and furnished a comfortable apartment for my parents and younger brother, right next door to where they lived, so they were immediately able to settle down and get comfortable in their new environment.

Unfortunately, a few days later, my mother took ill again with the usual symptoms—migraines, nausea, and vomiting. After a thorough examination, her new doctor assured her there was nothing to worry

Chapter 16

about. She took all the prescribed medicines, and after a few days was apparently cured of her ailments. The doctor told her to keep on taking the medicine—which she did scrupulously. Meanwhile, my father found work, initially in construction and subsequently at a gold processing company. Brother Ignazio enrolled in school, and after a few more days of visiting, Gioacchino and I returned to Montreal to get back to work. In the meantime, my parents began the process that would allow us to immigrate and join them in the U.S.

From time to time, I would telephone *alla Signorina* Pina to see how she was doing. I knew I really loved her, but I wasn't ready to disclose my feelings, and pretended I was merely making friendly conversation. On one particular occasion, I was filled with a desire to see her. She and her sister were living with her aunt and uncle at the time. Since I had never expressed my intentions, such a visit would have been considered improper, so I invented a pretext. I had received from the Quebec Department of Education the equivalency certificate for my Italian diploma. I asked her to explain what the certificate meant. As if I didn't know!

One Sunday afternoon, after gathering all my courage, I appeared at her doorstep, certificate in hand. I knocked at the door, and her aunt appeared. I asked if I could speak with Pina. As soon as I saw her, I was so overtaken by her presence that I was willing to be taken for an ignoramus who couldn't read the French equivalent of his own diploma—just so I could experience that delightful moment. Under her aunt's watchful eye, I showed Pina my certificate, asking if she could explain what it meant.

After reading it, she looked at me with a smile. "Exactly what is it you don't understand?" she asked facetiously.

"I'm not sure," I responded, genuinely unsure.

So, patiently, she explained what the certificate was all about.

Pretending to be suddenly enlightened, I thanked her for her help and left.

A few months later, Pina called me, saying her father had moved

Pina in 1968.

Chapter 16

to Montreal and that she and her sister were living with him in a rented apartment. She gave me her phone number, and I began to call her with some regularity, never revealing anything about how I felt about her. I simply didn't feel psychologically ready to do so—regardless of how deeply I loved her.

In February of 1969, I went to work for a company that sold mutual funds. While working there, I became close friends with a young Italian fellow named Gioacchino Arduini. The sale of mutual funds didn't prove profitable, so by the end of April my brother Gioacchino and I decided to move to Winnipeg, where, according to our cousin, there was plenty of work available in the construction industry.

This time I knew I couldn't leave for another city without disclosing my love to Pina. Afraid to confront her in person, I telephoned her.

"What would you think of the two of us getting married?" I asked.

Surprised by the abrupt way in which I handled such a delicate matter, she said she would need some time to think about it and asked if I had been considering the proposal for some time.

"Since the moment I saw you in the French class," I said.

The next day, after she had consulted her family, she telephoned. "I love you very much, Paolo, and I would be proud to be Mrs. Ficara."

That was all I needed to hear. I told her to hang up, because I was coming over. When I reached her house, I was so excited that words would not come. I simply hugged her tenderly for what seemed like a very long time.

No degree of happiness could match what I felt at that moment. I had found the one person in the entire world with whom I would share my dreams and goals, joys and sorrows, successes and failures—for the rest of my life.

Pina said she shared my vision of life and that she loved me sincerely for what I was, not for what I could be, and for what I had, not for what I could offer her in the future. She said she would follow me wherever I went, giving me all the help and support I needed, under any circumstances.

A few days later Gioacchino and I left for Winnipeg, where, with the help of my friend Leonardo Cacciatore, we found work as laborers for a construction company at two dollars and eighty-five cents an hour—good pay at the time, and enough to allow me to start saving money.

On July 30, the American consulate issued the visa that allowed me to enter the United Sates as an immigrant. Gioacchino would have his visa in a few more weeks.

After stopping in Montreal to visit for a few days with Pina, I took the bus to Waterbury. As soon as the bus reached the U.S. border patrol, an immigration officer boarded and checked passports of foreigners and driver licenses of Americans. When he reached me, he instructed me to get off the bus for further inspection.

My heart pounded as I followed his instructions. After a short wait inside the office, another officer asked to see all my documents, which he coldly and carefully examined. I was nervous during the entire process. After approximately ten minutes, he stamped my passport and then, with a smile on his face, said, "Welcome to the United States of America, and good luck to you."

It is impossible to express in words what I felt in my heart at that moment—so great was my joy. I managed to blabber, "Thank you." Then I slowly returned to the bus with a grin on my face.

After three long years of struggle and sacrifice, the first part of our dream was about to become a reality. Soon all the family would be reunited in a place where we could prosper and fulfill the rest of our dreams.

As soon the bus departed and was moving southbound on Interstate 87, I relaxed. Glancing out the window, I admired the landscape of my newly adopted country. Thoughts of Grandfather Paolo came to mind—all those things he told me about America when I was a kid. In particular I remember him telling me that America is the land of opportunity and possibility—the land where honesty and hard work for the most part allowed people to reach and live their dream. I would have given anything to have him there with me right then, even for just a few minutes. Never did those familiar words hold more meaning to me than in that moment.

"VOLERE, SIGNIFICA POTERE!"
(To Want Means To Be Able To!)

I was now living proof that no matter how difficult the task or how illusive our goals, when we apply every bit of our willpower and determination without giving up, we can reach our objectives.

Then I thought about all the strange events that had led me to this moment. One of the most defining was the 1968 earthquake in Sicily. That catastrophe triggered the mechanism that allowed my parents and brother to move to Waterbury—and now Gioacchino and me. If that earthquake had not occurred, the American president would not have issued the decree allowing Italians to immigrate to the U.S. And we likely wouldn't have had the good fortune of finding ourselves in America.

Again, I could not help but take note of the irony of such a disaster—how it destroys some lives, yet rejuvenates others.

So, the first part of my goal had been reached. Now there remained the second one:

Attain a reasonably good economic status in life.
Where could I begin?

From the time I had arrived in Montreal, I tried to find the kind of work I would most like to do, something that would ultimately allow me to achieve my goals and dreams.

After thinking it over for a long time, I reached the conclusion that construction work attracted me the most. I found it particularly interesting to work in the preparation and construction of roads, parking lots, and the laying of asphalt. I thought, once having learned the trade, our family could start a company of our own with relatively little capital. Then and there on Interstate 87, it dawned on me to look for work with an asphalt paving company. During my apprenticeship, I would try to save money and learn English, which would be indispensable to my running a company in the United States.

After about ten hours of travel, I reached Waterbury, where my parents, Ignazio, and all my aunts and uncles awaited me at the bus station. Two weeks later, Gioacchino would arrive as well.

It was August 1969, approximately five years after I had originally formulated my goal of uniting my family in one permanent place. Now the dream was a reality, and our collective joy was immense.

The evening I arrived, we had supper at Aunt Carmela's house. Afterwards, Uncle Salvatore's three brothers, Joe, Agostino and Luca, who spoke some Italian, came to visit.

"What kind of work would you like to do?" one of the brothers asked.

"I—"

"He will get a job at the factory," Aunt Carmela said.

"But I don't want to work in a factory." I replied.

"Yes, you do," Aunt Carmela insisted. "You'll have good pay and good benefits."

"I want to work for an asphalt paving company," I said. "I want to learn the trade so I can someday start my own business."

Aunt Carmela leaned back and stared at me. "Your own business? You just got here, and already, you want to be Mr. Business Owner?"

"Calm down," one of my uncle's brothers said. "It's okay. Just because me and my brothers have worked in the factories our whole lives doesn't mean Paolo must do the same." He turned to me. "You do what you want to do. Don't let anyone tell you what you want to do."

Aunt Carmela grunted, and she returned to her meal.

Chapter 16 123

When Paolo and Gioacchino first settled in Waterbury, Conn. in 1969, they joined thier parents and lived on the third floor of this triplex.

From left: Luca, his wife Connie, Joe, & Agostino Piazza, Zio (uncle) Salvatore's brothers. Waterbury, Conn. in 1969.

"And Paolo," he said, "right down on the next street is a company. Perazzini Construction. First generation Italian owns it. You just might want to check it out."

"Thank you." I smiled for the first time in this conversation. "Thank you," I repeated. "I will do that." At seven the next morning, accompanied by Ignazio, who acted as my interpreter, I went to Perazzini Construction, where I spoke with the owner's son. He told me I could begin work the next day at three-fifty an hour. Ignazio and I returned home to report the happy news to our parents.

That was an unforgettable day for me—not only because I was laying the foundation for my future, but also because I was going to earn three dollars and fifty cents an hour. Now I could save money for the future—something I had not been able to do in Canada.

Chapter 16

*Paolo's Youngest Brother Ignazio with Parents. 1970
First Family Car a 1970 Dodge Dart. Waterbury, Conn.*

CHAPTER 17
First Job, Engagement, First Business

The first few weeks of work were excruciatingly hard on me—both physically and emotionally. The August heat and the furnace-like atmosphere caused by the burning asphalt caused me to sweat profusely. My muscles, unused to such hard labor, ached day and night. A major conflict raged inside my head. Part of me said this work was not meant for me and I should find something less physically taxing. But the dominating part of me was convinced this was something I had to endure if I wanted to realize my lifelong dream.

During those moments of greatest stress, I became emotional, not knowing whether to laugh or cry—whether to abandon everything or to continue along with my plan. One day at work, I reached the peak of emotional turmoil. I actually thought I was going crazy, and in that precise moment from the deepest point of my heart, I knew I could not go on as I had been. Somehow, I managed to calm myself down and dismiss the negative thoughts that haunted me. Then I said to myself that it was time to look reality in the face and accept it—it was already too late to turn back the clock.

I told my muscles and my brain to get used to their fate, no matter the cost. After approximately three weeks of this turmoil I began to tire less quickly and felt more at ease. Noticing these changes, I gathered my courage and realized I had probably overcome the most difficult part of my trial. I found myself looking forward to going to work in the morning.

It took me about three months to become accustomed to the mind-set of a laborer. During that time my muscles became stronger, and

Chapter 17

Pina and Paolo on their engagement party, December, 1969.

1969 Christmas Party with family.
From the right to the left: Brother Gioacchino, my Father, my Mother, Pina, myself, brother Ignazio and Pina's Father. Waterbury, Conn.

Chapter 17

my burden seemed lighter. I appreciated more what I was doing. Not only was I happier, but I also felt pride in my hard work. With my new frame of mind, I was able to accomplish my tasks with greater enthusiasm and use my capabilities to their utmost.

In the meanwhile, Gioacchino found work as a gardener. Ignazio was going to school. My father worked in a factory, and my mother took care of the household. In the evenings and on my days off, I spent most of my time writing long letters to Pina, who now worked for a clothing manufacturer in Montreal and taught Italian in a local school on Saturdays. Thus, we all lived in harmony, getting on perfectly in accordance with our life's plans.

My bank account grew steadily, and towards the end of December, we bought a new car—a four-door Dodge Dart.

For Christmas 1969, the family went to Montreal to spend the holidays with my fiancée. Pina and I decided to get married, and we set the date for the twelfth of December 1970.

One day during our stay in Montreal, I became irritated by something my fiancée had said to me. Cramps gripped my intestines and I couldn't eat. After Pina and I realized our misunderstanding was over trifles and cleared the air, we had a laugh and went out to eat at a good restaurant, where we drank wine and toasted our love, happiness, and future. It took a few days, but the cramps eventually dissipated.

Immediately after the holidays, I returned to Waterbury, where I continued with my work. With nothing to do to occupy my time, I was getting bored in the evenings and weekends. I suggested to Gioacchino that it might be wise to get a part-time job—something that would not only allow us to be more productive with our free time but would put additional money in our pockets.

A few days later over supper, Gioacchino said he had spoken with the owner of the company where he worked, who suggested we try gardening. The owner said many people, either because of advanced age or a busy working schedule, were not able to care for their gardens, and if we placed an ad in the local paper, we were bound to find all the work we wanted.

We agreed it was a brilliant idea. But there was a problem—neither Gioacchino nor I could speak English. How could we communicate with people? Who would answer the phone and take messages? Ignazio suggested we specify in our ad that calls would be accepted after five in the afternoon—since that was when he was at home studying, and he could answer the phone. Furthermore, he would be able to accompany us to meet with potential customers and act as our interpreter. In order to put this idea into practice, we had to wait for spring. With the heavy snowfalls, no one was thinking about lawns or gardens.

Since my return from Montreal, I noticed that after meals—especially if I drank a glass of beer or ate nuts—my stomach swelled like a balloon, and I felt bloated. My folks tried to convince me to see a doctor, but I refused, saying there was no need for it. Then, one evening, around the end of February, pain cramped through my heart. It was difficult for me to breathe. That was when I began to worry.

The following day, accompanied by Ignazio, I went to see a doctor, who examined me, sent me for x-rays, and concluded I had a stomach ulcer. When I asked him what might have caused it, he replied there were many reasons, but the most common was nervousness and worry.

"Nothing to worry about, Paolo. Eat right and take the medication, and in time, the ulcer will heal. You'll be fine."

Relieved by the diagnosis, Ignazio and I went straight home to reassure our parents, who had been concerned.

Every time I took the prescribed pills, I became sleepy—to the point of feeling drunk. Considering the nature of my job, drowsiness was dangerous. After a week, I went back to the doctor and explained my new symptoms. He said I was having a normal reaction to the drug—and there was nothing to worry about. When I asked how long it would take me to get well, he replied he did not know.

The doctor's vague answers left me quite perplexed, especially

Chapter 17

My father and I at our first job as gardeners, Waterbury, Conn. April first 1970.

considering of the difficulty I was encountering with my work. Regardless of the doctor's opinion, I knew if I continued to take the pills and work at the same time, sooner or later I would get hurt—and the only way I could continue the treatment was by giving up my job. Since that was not an option, I decided to take the pills only at bedtime. Meanwhile, I noticed that what I ate affected how I felt. So I stopped taking the pills all together, never went back to the doctor and simply paid attention to my diet. That did the job, and in time I was healed.

The radiologist, who had taken my x-rays a few weeks before, was of Italian origin and spoke some Italian. He asked me about the kind of work I did, and I replied that I was working in construction—but come spring, I planned to do part-time gardening with my brothers. I confided that I was getting married in December, and could use the extra money. He encouraged me and asked for an estimate to clean his yard.

On the last Saturday of March, after the snow had melted, my brothers, my father, and I went to the radiologist's house to take a look at his yard. We estimated the cost to clean it at twenty dollars. The radiologist gave his approval, and so, full of excitement, the following Saturday we went to his home. Because of our limited experience, we thought the work would take us only an hour or so—but we had underestimated the time required. In fact, it took us almost eight hours to do that job. After we finished, the radiologist came out and complimented us on our work. To show his satisfaction, he even added a five-dollar tip.

On the way home, we estimated we had worked for approximately seventy-eight cents an hour, but instead of being irritated for having worked practically for nothing, we were euphoric. We were twenty-five dollars richer than if we had stayed home doing nothing. On top of that, we'd had an experience to remember.

Now that we knew how much work we could accomplish in a given time, we had a better idea of how to price our next job. Little by little, with Ignazio's help, we acquired many customers and worked every evening until dark, including Saturdays and Sundays.

We worked long hours, but this part-time activity proved to be indispensable—it allowed me to save some money for my imminent wedding and later allowed us to provide our family everything they needed to overcome the financial difficulties we had gone through.

During the fifties and sixties, Waterbury underwent a period of economic development, after which the area went into decline. I noticed that labor unions had a greater voice in the way things were run, often giving headaches to companies and creating conditions that were not exactly ideal for a flourishing economy. Once the companies lost competitive strength, they laid off employees, often closing down plants and moving to other states with more favorable conditions. The construction industry followed the fluctuations of the general economy and underwent an equally critical period.

I realized how difficult it would be to reach my goals. Once again, I went through a period of confusion and uncertainty. During the month of June, 1970, Pina came to Waterbury to spend a week with me and to attend the wedding of one of Uncle Salvatore's nephews.

During her stay, I confided my worries. If my plans and goals were to be realized, I would have to move back to Canada. Of course, such a move would mean leaving my family once again, which was a dismal prospect. Nevertheless, I suggested that after getting married, we should stay in Waterbury for one year—we could live with my parents and save the funds needed to get me started as a contractor. After that, we would move to Calgary, Alberta—which was experiencing more development than any other city in Canada—the perfect place to realize our goals.

Pina fully agreed with me. She said she loved me and would follow me anywhere. "You make me so happy," she assured me, "that any sacrifice I make for us is not a burden, but a joy."

My heart was full of gratitude for having found a woman who loved me for myself, and not for what I could do for her. Our love for each other was in no way conditioned by material things, but was an end in itself. With a woman like Pina by my side, I knew I could reach any goal I desired. Her help, her understanding, and her devotion were the best medicine my young heart could ever have hoped to find.

Chapter 17

Paolo & Pina Wedding Picture
December 12, 1970 – Waterbury, Conn.

CHAPTER 18
Marriage

The year 1970 was one of the happiest of my life. Work was going well, and when I wasn't working, I spent much of my time talking with my father, who related the most significant experiences of his life. These frequent discussions proved enormously important for me, not only because they allowed me to get to know my father in a new way, but also because each story conveyed a message of wisdom which opened my mind and heart to life's greatest challenges.

The stories, often told in parables, strengthened my character, developed my understanding, and helped me grasp in a practical way what life was all about. On those occasions he always reminded me that love for the family and loyalty to friends and employers are the things that lead to a good and happy life. My heart overflowed with joy and gratitude for my father's deep love and respect for my mother, my brothers and myself, and for his uncommon qualities.

And finally, when my thoughts turned to my Pina, whom the good Lord had brought into my life, I felt as though I were living in a dream world—such was my bliss.

By the end of October, I realized I didn't have sufficient funds to cover all my wedding expenses. While speaking with my father and brothers one evening, I mentioned I had to get a loan from the bank. They unanimously replied that there was no need to ask for a loan, since I could use the money we had accumulated that summer working as gardeners. I said it wasn't right for me to let them go through any further financial sacrifices on my account. What they had done to help me in the past was more than enough.

Chapter 18 137

*December 12, 1970 – More Wedding Pictures
From the right to the left: My father, my mother, myself, Pina,
Pina's mother and Pina's father.*

*December 12, 1970 – Wedding Picture.
My mother and her sister, Zia (aunt) Carmela.*

December 12, 1970 – Wedding Picture
From the right to the left: Brother Ignazio, cousin Mariella, Myself, Pina, Pina's Sister Paola, and my brother Gioacchino.

December 12, 1970 – Wedding Picture
From the right to the left: My father, my Mother, Myself, Pina, Zia (aunt) Carmela, and Zio (uncle) Salvatore.

Chapter 18

*Our wedding church, Our Lady of Lourds
in South Main Street, Waterbury, Conn.*

*My father-in-law walking Pina down the isle to the Alter.
12 December 1970, Waterbury, Conn.*

Chapter 18

Christmas Celebration in Ribera 1970 – while on our honeymoon. From the right to the left: Zio (uncle) Lillo, my father's young brother, myself, my father, Pina, cousin Gioacchino and cousin Antonio (Zio Lillo's sons).

Left to right is Zio (uncle) Lillo, Zia (aunt) Lina, Zia (aunt) Antonietta and Pina. Christmas in Ribera 1970.

Christmas in Ribera 1970.
From the left: Zio (uncle) Lillo, Zia (aunt) Fina (my father's younger sister), my father, Cousin Rosa and Cousin Ignazio DiGrado.

Chapter 18

Despite my protests, my father firmly assured me the family would take care of everything. Extremely touched by their kindness and generosity, I expressed my sincere gratitude.

In early November, Pina and her mother came to Waterbury. Together, we made the necessary preparations for the wedding, which took place on December 12. The service was beautiful, and we were honored and delighted by the presence of our friends and relatives who attended—many of whom had come a great distance.

On the day following the wedding, my father and Gioacchino left for Italy, as my father wanted to spend the Christmas holidays with his family. He told us he had to do so while they were still alive and in good health—because only God knew what might happen from one day to the next.

Pina and I remained in Waterbury for another three days, and then left for our honeymoon in Italy, where my wife wanted me to meet her two brothers. Our first stop was Rome, where my brother-in-law Mercurio was awaiting us. Thereafter, we proceeded to Milano, visiting the city and its surroundings. After a few days, we flew to Sicilia, stopping in Ribera, where my father, brother, and all our friends and relatives waited for us. After having been away for a few years, I felt elated to be surrounded by aunts, uncles, friends, and relatives with whom I had spent my youth.

The town of Cattolica Eraclea was only about ten miles from Ribera. Since it was my wife's hometown, we visited often, spending most of our time in the homes of friends and relatives who invited us daily for dinner or to parties in our honor. My old friends Giuseppe Zabbara and Enzo Tortorici came to visit us almost every evening, and we reminisced about old times. Another friend, Franco Sferra, also spent most of his free time with us, telling us about his life since I'd left Ribera.

Salvatore Palumbo invited us to dinner one night and admitted he had underestimated my ability to reach my goals. "I'm so happy to see you have achieved your first dream—you've succeeded in getting

Pina in Ribera at the family orange groves – Christmas 1970.

your family together," he said. "I feel confident your second one will follow."

This time around, having experienced my share of setbacks, I chose to play the devil's advocate, and explained the difficulties in reaching the lofty goal of owning my own business. "Difficult, but not impossible," I said.

Everyone concurred, and we all drank a toast to our collective health and success.

A few days before Christmas, my brother-in-law Andrea arrived from Sardegna (Sardinia), where he was teaching, to spend the holidays with us. After New Year's Day, he had to return to work but told us we could use his car during our honeymoon as long as we brought it back to him in Sardegna before we returned to the U.S. We accepted his offer, in part, because it was going to give us the chance to see and visit this beautiful highland.

When Pina and I arrived in Ribera, we noticed my father was quite perturbed—even though he tried to pretend everything was fine. One day, I asked him to go for a walk with me to the *piazza principale*. As we walked, I asked him what was wrong. After some hesitation, he told me his sisters and brothers were upset because he had not brought them expensive gifts from America. In their minds, their brother had become very rich in the U.S. and was therefore expected to share some of his wealth with the rest of the family. Since this had not turned out to be the case, they received him coldly or indifferently, not even bothering to invite him to their homes for dinner.

This reaction of his family deeply hurt my father, as it went completely against his idealistic code of conduct. They had denigrated the very principles of generosity that he held sacred in life. He believed the most important and the greatest gift he could ever give them was himself—being there with them for the holidays—and any other outward manifestation should have been viewed as having little or no consequence.

My father's relatives could not even fathom the financial sacrifices he'd gone through in order to save enough money for the trip; nor did they understand the risks involved in undertaking such a long journey at his age. None of them noticed that neither distance nor time had in any way changed the deep love he bore them. That love was the only reason for his return to Ribera.

From my father's viewpoint, these were simple-minded creatures whose hearts had become hardened and whose brains were only absorbed by the egotistical, material trifles of life. They mistook outward appearances for the true brotherhood and respect that should govern human relationships.

As he spoke, he looked into my eyes. "Remember never to fall into the same trap when you have a family of your own."

At age twenty-five, I was receiving one of the greatest lessons in life from my illiterate father—that none of my highly educated instructors in all my years of schooling had not been able to teach me.

A few days following that conversation, my father got together with my brother and me. He told us the events of the last few days had offended him to the point of disgust. After what had happened, he decided he wanted to sell all his property in Ribera. Gioacchino and I told him we would not consider living in Ribera again, and if selling the property would make him happy, we supported him in his decision.

He began to divest himself of his property by trying to sell a plot of land that Grandfather Paolo had given in dowry to my mother upon her marriage. At the time my father had departed for the U.S., he had left this plot to a cousin of his—with the understanding he could cultivate the land and keep the profits, but if my father wanted it back, he would not ask for compensation of any kind. At that time, the cousin had promised there would be no problem—that my father's land was his to do with as he chose.

So, in order to facilitate the sale of the plot, my father went to see his cousin and told him of his intentions. The cousin said he would like to buy the land, but only at half the market value. He argued he was

Chapter 18

supposed to have received an indemnity for having worked the land during the preceding two years. He stated further that if my father did not accept his conditions, he would not relinquish his "legal" rights to the property. My father reminded him of his promise, and that he had not asked him for a single penny over the course of the previous two years.

"I've changed my mind. And as far as you're concerned, you would be wise to accept my offer, since my attorney tells me the law is on my side."

My father was furious at this breach of good faith and vowed to fight for his land even if it meant incurring more in legal expenses than the value of the land. Accordingly, he started legal proceedings against his cousin. Seeing that my father meant business, his cousin agreed to pay the fair market value of the property. Despite my father's outward calm, I could see the incident had shaken him badly. It was a rude awakening for me, as well, as I preferred to believe that love and respect for humanity should always supersede love for material things.

As soon as the holidays were over, Gioacchino and my father returned to the U.S., while Pina and I drove Andrea's car to Catania, where my father-in-law's sister and her family resided. They received us with all the warmth and affection anybody could ask for. One of my wife's cousins, Angelina, took time off from work just to keep us company and show us around Catania and the surrounding areas. We remained there for about a week, during which time we saw Mount Etna, Taormina, Ragusa, Siracusa, and their major archaeological sites.

We then proceeded to Messina, where we took the ferry to the mainland to visit Calabria. After that, our whirlwind tour of Italy included spending three days in Napoli visiting Amalfi, Sorrento, and Pompeii—as well as Nocera Inferiore, where I showed Pina the barracks in which I spent ten months of my military life. Skipping Rome because we had both been there previously, we drove north to

Florence, where we visited two dear friends of my mother, the ones I saw on my way back from my first trip to Germany. We stayed in Toscana (Tuscany) for five days, visited the famous Leaning Tower of Pisa, and then went on to Venezia (Venice) and its extraordinary canals and architectural splendors. Next, we saw Verona, where we visited a family with whom my father had stayed for nearly two years during World War II.

Milano and a few days with Mercurio were our next stop. While there, we visited several nearby places, including Lugano in Switzerland, which we found positively enchanting. From there we spent two days in Genova as guests of my cousin Gioacchino and his family. From Genova, we took the ferryboat to Sardegna. Andrea acted as our guide as we discovered the beauty of that wonderful island—similar in so many ways to my native Sicily, so rich in sunlight with white, glittering beaches. After touring Sardegna, we left for Montreal to spend a few days with Pina's parents and sister.

Tired, homesick, and with only ten dollars remaining in our pockets, Pina and I returned to Waterbury, Connecticut, on February 10, 1971—two months after we had left. One of the most splendid chapters of our lives was now history.

The future lay ahead of us.

CHAPTER 19
Father's Illness

Soon after arriving back home, I learned my father was not feeling well. Immediately following his return from Ribera, he had begun to experience severe headaches. The treatment prescribed by the physician proved ineffective, and the cause remained unknown. I suggested we contact another doctor and get a second opinion. I called Zio *(uncle)* Joe, Zio *(uncle)* Salvatore's brother for a recommendation. He recommended his family doctor, an Italian-American named Joe Bizozzaro, who was a professor at the Yale University Medical School in nearby New Haven.

Full of hope, I asked if he could book us an appointment for the next day. Five minutes later he called back to say the doctor could not schedule a normal appointment anytime soon, but if we would be willing to come to the office on the following day and wait until they could free up some time, my father would get his examination.

On the next day, I took my father to see Dr. Bizozzaro. After a long wait, the nurse called us in to an examination room. A few minutes later, the doctor came in, smiling. As we shook hands, he asked my father in Italian the nature of his problem. Happy to hear the doctor conversant in Italian, my father spoke freely about his symptoms.

While my father talked, the doctor observed him closely and listened to every word he said. Then, he went on to examine my father's neck. After a few moments' reflection, he said he would have to admit my father to the hospital for three days of diagnostic testing. The doctor added that his nurse would contact the hospital and make all the necessary arrangements for admission.

Just as we were at the front door, ready to leave, the nurse called me and told me the doctor had forgotten to ask me something. I went back into the doctor's office. When I entered, the doctor said he had not wanted to talk to me in front of my father. Then, with a rather perplexed look, he explained that during the examination he found a growth on my father's neck, which none of us had noticed before. He thought it could be a tumor, possibly malignant, and for that reason had ordered a biopsy on the tissue.

"In the meantime," he told me in Italian, "*non ti preoccupare* (do not worry and hope for the best)."

When I returned, my father asked me what the doctor had to say.

"He just wanted to know the name of your insurance company," I answered. I didn't want him to know the truth.

As soon we got home, we were bombarded with questions from my mother and brothers. I said the doctor wanted to perform some routine tests at the hospital, but he assured me there was nothing to worry about. That evening I took Gioacchino out for a walk and filled him in on everything the doctor told me.

A few days later, my father was admitted to the hospital, where the tests were performed. After they were completed, he was told the results would be sent directly to the doctor, who in turn would notify him.

The day before we got the results, I had a strange dream in which my father and Uncle Lillo each appeared to have a long, thick thorn embedded in one of their legs. In an effort to deliver them from excruciating pain, I extracted the thorns. Uncle Lillo gave out a sigh of relief and began to walk, but my father closed his eyes and showed no signs of life. I screamed and sobbed. Shaking him with vengeance, I begged him to speak to me. But he lay lifeless, and there was nothing I could do to restore his breathing. I woke up, waking Pina in the process. She asked me what was going on. Still sobbing, I related the dream, adding that we would not be able to help my father and that he was going to die very soon.

Chapter 19

"It was only a dream, sweetheart," Pina said. "My mother always said that if you dream of death, it means long life."

I wanted to believe her with all my heart, but something inside me said otherwise. "He's not going to get well. I can feel it."

"Nonsense," she assured me. "The doctor is bound to find a cure for him. Medical science is doing amazing things these days. You'll see I'm right."

Then she turned on her side and tried to sleep, but I heard her moving about, restless. Neither of us slept the rest of the night. We waited until the crack of dawn and then jumped out of bed.

That morning, we received a letter from Aunt Lina, Uncle Lillo's wife, in which she informed us that Uncle Lillo had been ill with kidney stones and had to be admitted to the hospital. But fortunately, thanks to the use of appropriate drugs and good medical care, he had recovered in a relatively short time and was now very well.

In the afternoon of that same day, my father's doctor's secretary telephoned, asking me to come to the doctor's office. That's when I got the bad news. Dr. Bizozzaro was sorry to tell me the tests had confirmed his worst suspicions—we were dealing with a malignant tumor.

In my attempt to disconnect from the harsh reality, I clenched my teeth. "That can't be. He's only got headaches. He's not really sick."

The doctor remained silent while I regained my composure. "Don't worry. The battle's not over yet. There's a surgical procedure that could make a difference. We won't know, of course, until we go in."

"I will discuss the matter with my family, tell them what you recommend, and I'll let you know how they want to proceed." Then I thanked him and left.

Back in my car, I felt as though I were losing my mind. I sat behind the wheel and cried uncontrollably—wondering why such a terrible thing had to happen precisely at the moment our dream had become a reality—when the whole family was finally living together under one roof, with a bright future before us.

Defiance surged towards that something I couldn't see—and whose existence I often doubted. I was furious with the entity we refer to as God, believing He was being unfair.

- **Why would God allow misery, pain, and sickness to pervade our lives?**

Once again, I found myself with no answers and no way to understand His ways. Once again I began to doubt:
- **His goodness**
- **His love**
- **His mercy**
- **His justice**
- **His very existence**

I continued to cry, just like a child who's lost his most beautiful and cherished toy. Yes, indeed, I was losing my best and dearest friend, the greatest teacher I had ever known, the person who had given me everything he could without ever asking for anything in return. I was losing my father. The prophecy of the previous night's dream was beginning to manifest.

After getting a hold on myself, I started the car and went to pick up Pina from work. When she saw my red eyes and dismal expression, she asked what had happened. I related that I had spoken with the doctor, but before I could finish the sentence, tears ran down my cheeks. She realized what was happening and hugged me in an effort to share my pain and help me endure my grief. We drove home without saying another word.

When we arrived home, I parked the car, and after regaining control of my emotions, we went inside. Everyone's eyes were on me, trying to interpret my expression. "What did the doctor say?" they wanted to know.

I chose to make it easier on everyone, saying, "It's nothing serious.

The doctor wants to perform minor surgery to remove the growth, that's all."

They all heaved a deep sigh of relief. My father proposed I make arrangements with the doctor to schedule surgery as soon as possible. I nodded my assent, and we ate supper. Afterwards, my brothers agreed to accompany me to the market, ostensibly to buy some fruit. Inside the car I explained the facts. Naturally, my brothers were shocked by the gravity of the situation.

"We must confront this problem with calm and determination," I said, "standing firmly united in our common goal to support one another. Most of all, we need to keep alive those same ideals our father continues to inculcate in our hearts and minds." I paused and took a deep breath. "Otherwise, we run the risk of losing our mother."

The following day I called Dr. Bizozzaro and told him we were prepared to go along with his recommendations. To begin with, we were to accompany my father every day for ten weeks to the Yale University Hospital in New Haven, which was about a one hour drive each way, so he could undergo special radiation treatments. This procedure would reduce the tumor's size and allow the surgery to be performed with greater ease.

When my father found out he had to commute to New Haven every day, he was extremely discouraged, as he could neither drive nor find an alternate means of transportation. I told him not to worry, since I would be accompanying him. He argued that I was a married man now, and that I had to carry on with my work and take care of my new family.

I looked him in the eye, and with all the love and respect I could express, I said, "Nothing is more important to me at this moment than you. Not work, not money, not anything. After all, are you not my family?"

Tears welled up in his eyes, and he said he did not want to become a nuisance to anyone. I told him to stop worrying and to start thinking about getting well as soon as possible. A few days later we began our

Paolo with parents after his father's first surgery in Waterbury, Conn. 1972.

Father and Brother Ignazio – in 1972.

Chapter 19

daily trips to the hospital for radiation.

It was April. Now that the snow was gone and vegetation sprouted in fields and gardens, my brothers and I resumed our part-time work as gardeners evenings and weekends. Thanks to the extra income, we were able to keep our family's standard of living at a reasonable level without anyone suffering much in the way of comfort or financial security.

Meanwhile, I noticed that Pina wasn't comfortable living with the rest of the family. The physical proximity sometimes gave rise to minor misunderstandings. I told her to relax, assuring her that if my father got through the operation safely, as all of us hoped he would, then we could move to Calgary, where she could enjoy all the privacy her heart desired.

At the end of the ten weeks of therapy, my father felt better, allowing us to feel more optimistic about the future. Dr. Bizozzaro scheduled a date for the surgery. Before my father was admitted into the operating room, we asked the surgeon his chances for recovery. His reply was "fifty percent."

The operation was successful, but my father lost seventy percent mobility in his mouth due to nerve damage. He could no longer eat whatever he wanted and had to be content with milk, fruit juices and baby foods. Despite this limitation, he never gave in to despair. Most important, he no longer suffered from terrible headaches. Eventually he was able to work again, which pleased him immensely.

*Paolo and Pina with their friends Vincenzina and Filippo
Calgary, Christmas 1971.*

CHAPTER 20
Calgary and Waterbury

During the first days of September, 1971, my father was in relatively good shape and kept working with no apparent problems. Thinking the worst was over, Pina and I decided it was time to move to Calgary. Filled our pockets with our savings and our hearts with hope, we undertook the trip to the Canadian city. Once there, we lived for a few days with some old friends from Ribera, Vincenzina and her husband Filippo.

Calgary was a beautiful, modern city, undergoing a phase of significant commercial expansion. Imposing projects under construction appeared everywhere we turned—a fact that filled our hearts with joy, since it seemed apparent we had arrived at the right time. Pina immediately found employment with a uniform manufacturing firm, while I was able to join my friends who were employed by a large construction company specializing in the installation of water mains and sewers.

Approximately two weeks after our arrival, we purchased a new three-quarter ton, four-wheel drive GMC pickup, specially equipped with a frontal snow plough. Thanks to this contraption, we could earn extra income sweeping the snow in supermarket parking lots when snowing and the weather made it impossible to work in construction.

Around Christmas time, Pina and I deiced to have our first child.

We began trying to conceive, but nothing happened. Concerned, we went to see a gynecologist, who assured us we were both in perfect health and that we had to keep trying.

Time went sweetly by and we were already in the spring. My father was still working and feeling relatively well, and I had just left the construction company where I had been working, getting ready to organize my own firm. Around the end of April, we got the incredible news that Pina was pregnant. We were overwhelmed with excitement and joy. The thought of becoming a father along with the prospect of having my own company and of being my own boss gave me an extraordinary feeling of elation. My lifelong dream was about to come true.

After procuring a business license from the city, I advertised my company in the local newspaper. At the same time every day, I made a habit of driving around the city looking for houses that may need a driveway paved. Little by little I secured small contracts.

When I thought I had enough work to keep me busy, I bought a small dump truck and all the equipment I needed. Then I decided to hire two laborers.

That's when the difficulties of running a business emerged.

Because of the great construction boom in Calgary, everyone with experience in the building trade—and those who were inclined to work hard—were employed by large companies that offered good wages, fringe benefits, and steady jobs.

It was quite understandable to me that none of these workers would even consider switching over to my enterprise, which could offer them none of those things. Ultimately, I was forced to hire two inexperienced workers. This turn of events—plus the fact that I had no experience running a business—made it far more difficult to succeed than I imagined.

After the first month, I was able to draw a few conclusions. For one thing, I was earning more money than I'd ever earned working as a laborer. Although this seemed positive from a business standpoint, running a firm was not as simple as it might first appear. Organizing and managing an enterprise was a difficult and tedious task requiring far more work, responsibility, and resourcefulness than I had been accustomed to as an employee. This was particularly so in my case—starting from scratch, and in a place far from my loved ones, where I knew virtually no one, nor was I acquainted with the local milieu. To make matters worse, I

Chapter 20

Our First Pickup Truck equipped with a Snow Plow, Calgary, January 1972.

Pina in our friends garden – pregnant with our first child, Calgary, July, 1972.

could not get good and reliable workers.

My biggest problem was that in order to generate business I had to be constantly on the move, and this entailed an enormous expenditure of time and physical energy. On a typical day, I would get up at dawn and go pick up my workers at their respective homes. After working with them for eight to ten hours, I repeated the process and took them back home again. Then I went to visit prospective clients. I never got home before eight or nine o'clock in the evening. Once home, I had to answer phone messages, after which I was able to shower. Only then could Pina and I finally sit down for supper. And that was how we spent each day of the week, including Saturdays and Sundays.

Although I was still young, full of energy and endowed with the will to succeed, exhaustion was beginning to consume me. By the end of the second month, I realized I couldn't continue to work at such a breakneck pace. It was simply impossible.

I decided to make a thorough assessment of the situation and of my own capabilities. I was quite capable of working hard and was able to do whatever task was put before me. People developed a certain trust in me and listened to my advice. This helped me considerably in securing more contracts. I was also good at making correct estimates and calculating the right profit margins—consequently earning more from each job. On the whole, I was convinced I had the necessary prerequisites to lead a successful operation.

The only problem was that I could not do everything by myself.

I came to the conclusion that for me to be able to succeed in my business, I needed the help of an experienced worker capable of overseeing the job and the other workers, thereby freeing me to concentrate on my administrative duties.

During this period, I met a Sicilian named Giovanni Quartararo, married to a woman from my hometown of Ribera. This man had experience in the type of work I was doing and was currently employed by a large construction company. On occasion, whenever he had a Saturday off, he came to help me out. Since he seemed to be a good person as well as a capable worker, I proposed that he come work for me on a regular basis. I said I would share half the profits of my company with him—which was considerably more than he earned from his own employer.

He thanked me for my offer and the trust I showed in him, but he wanted to think it over. A few days later he told me he didn't want to quit his job—if things should not turn out as well as expected with my company, he would find himself out of work and without any likelihood of getting his old job back.

Not long after, I made the same proposal to my friend Filippo. This time the response was positive, so we began to work together. But the man did not have a driver's license, which became an added burden for me.

One evening, in the middle of September, I was on the phone with Gioacchino in Waterbury, explaining my frustrations to him—something I had avoided doing before to keep my family from worrying unnecessarily. He said he'd be happy to come up and help me out, but unfortunately, he couldn't.

I asked him why. After some hesitation, he told me the news I didn't want to hear. "Our father was complaining about the same old symptoms, so we took him back to the hospital. The tumor is back, but this time on the other side of his neck. He's going to need more surgery."

"Is he going to be all right, do you think?"

"This time the doctor is less hopeful, Paolo. I'm sorry," he said. "He's not expected to recover fully, and he will never be able to go back to work. I didn't tell you this earlier because there was nothing you could have done. I didn't see any point in worrying you."

At first, I was so shocked by the news I couldn't utter a word. After a moment of pulling myself together, I tried to console my brother—telling him not to fret and that I was counting on him to be strong for our mother and Ignazio.

Gioacchino's news weighed heavily on me. That night I got no sleep at all. My thoughts were with my father and all my other family members to whom, because of the distance separating us, I could neither offer a word of consolation nor give the least bit of personal support.

The days that followed were strenuous in every respect—made worse because I could no longer concentrate on my work. I lacked the courage and the drive to function as I had during the previous few months. I was filled with confusion and dread as I reflected on the cruelty of life and the capriciousness of fate.

As this turmoil was fomenting in my head, I asked myself the following questions:

- **What wrong had my father done to deserve such a harsh punishment?**
- **What terrible deed had I committed to warrant the trials and misfortunes I was going through?**
- **Why did God, assuming that He existed, allow all this to happen?**

Once again I received no answers to these burning questions.

I wondered if I should remain in Calgary or simply drop everything and go back to Waterbury and stay with my family—thus failing miserably in my effort to achieve security and financial success in Calgary. The answer came to me suddenly from the bottom of my heart and without ambiguity. The right thing to do was to return to Waterbury and assist my father during the last days of his life—and show that my love for him was as deep as the one he had borne for all of us—his family. This feeling, as far as I was concerned, superseded any thoughts of material or financial success. Moreover, by going back to Waterbury, I would have a chance to console my mother and brothers.

I discussed the situation with Pina. "Okay," she said, "as long as we can rent a little apartment of our own."

"That's a promise," I said with the best of intentions.

Immediately I stopped working and sold the dump truck. I told Pina that since she was six months pregnant, it would be best if she traveled

Chapter 20

to Waterbury by plane while I drove back in our new pickup truck. She adamantly refused, insisting she would never allow me to travel alone on such a long haul. I reminded her that traveling by truck on a 3,000-mile journey could be very risky, both for her and for the baby she was carrying. But, all to no avail. Pina was determined to come with me, and I consented.

The day we left for Waterbury, my father had his second operation. When we arrived there days later, he was still in the hospital recuperating, so we went to see him. He was as elated at the sight of us as we were of him. A few days later, he was discharged and allowed to return home.

In the meantime, Pina and I moved in with the family, as we had nowhere else to stay. Gioacchino asked the owner of his company if there was any work for me. The response was positive, and I was immediately hired at four-fifty an hour. Because she was in the late stages of pregnancy, Pina could not go to work, so she stayed home helping my mother with the household chores.

Approximately a month following our arrival, Pina reminded me of the promise I had made her regarding a place of our own. I told her that with winter approaching and the possibility of layoffs, the cost of furniture and a rented apartment would be a burden we could not afford.

"We can use our savings," she said. "This is extremely important to me, and even more so with our baby coming soon."

The savings we had accumulated were barely enough to pay the medical bills following the baby's delivery. As much as she tried to reason with me, I remained adamant. "We will stay with the family until we are absolutely sure we can pay our own way."

Why was I so stubborn, refusing to keep my promise?

Perhaps, because I worried too much.

Or, maybe because I was concerned for my father's health.

Or maybe because I was not as strong as I should have been.

Or maybe because I feared the uncertainty of the future.

To tell the truth, even today—after all these years—I don't really have the answer.

Maybe all those things contributed to me ignoring my wife's right to privacy, as well as that of my parents and my brothers. My behavior, whether due to lack of understanding or basic character weakness, was the worst I ever exhibited over the course of my life. Only now, these many years later, do I truly understand the impositions I placed on my wife and family during that complicated period of our lives. If I could live my life over, I would make every effort to avoid that particular error—at any cost.

As the days went by, Pina and I experienced the same conditions of stress and ill will that had characterized our relationship before we departed for Calgary.

She argued that I did not give her enough attention, and that she resented not being cuddled and appreciated for the things she did for me and for the family. Worst of all, she was hurt that I never told her I loved her. This lack of basic communication eventually led to many misunderstandings and made her doubt my devotion to her.

I tried to make her understand that if I did not express in words what I felt in my heart, it was not out of malice or indifference, but simply because it was my nature. "You must have noticed that I behave similarly with my family. It's the way we are. We find no reason to express in words what our hearts already know—that our love is unconditional, and that words cannot begin to express the depth of our feelings."

Chapter 20

Pina with our first child Pellegrino Pino Ficara who is 3 days old.

Pellegrino Pino at 2 months old.

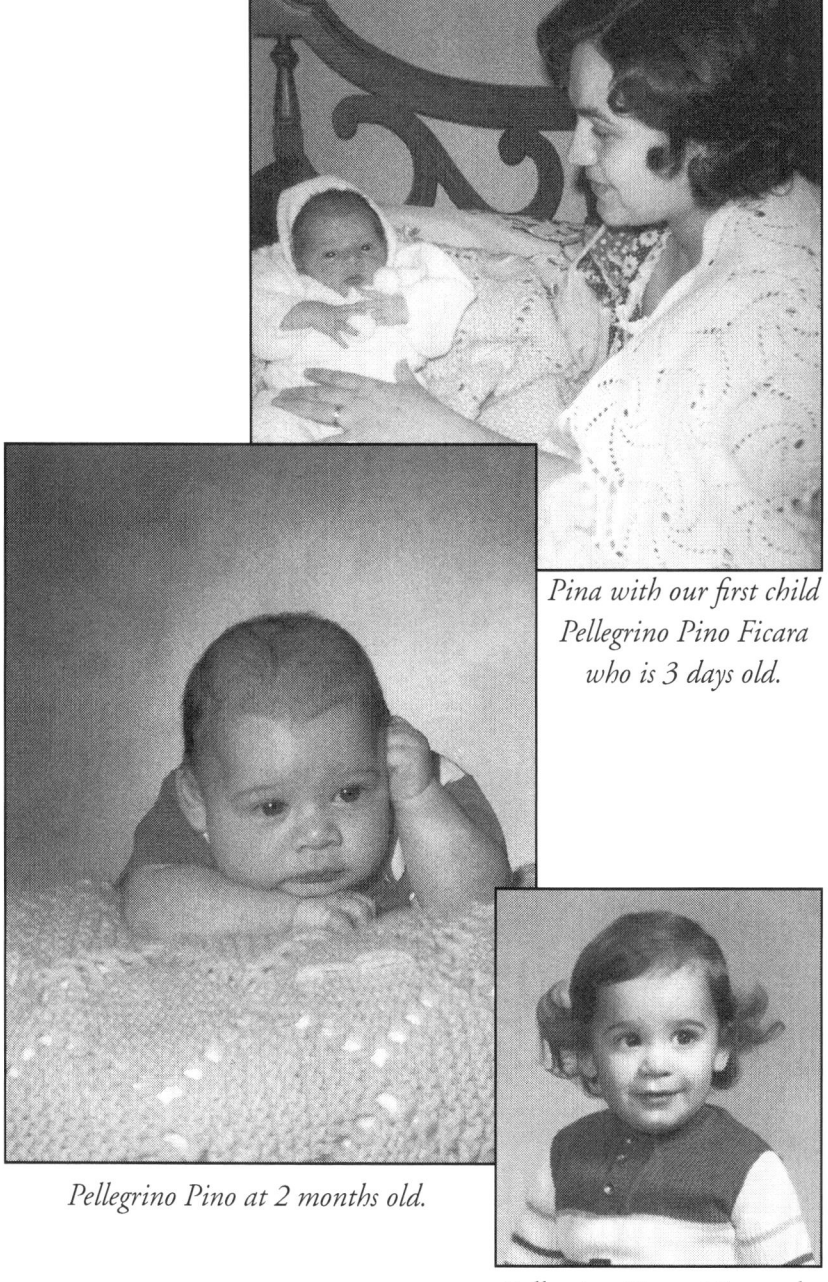

Pellegrino Pino –16 months old.

CHAPTER 21
First Child, First Home

In the midst of all of this conflict, our first-born baby arrived. The night of December 30, 1972, Pina gave birth to our beautiful boy. Pellegrino (Pino) was named for my father, in accordance with tradition. His arrival brought joy into our hearts, but the atmosphere in which Pina and I lived remained unchanged. We continued to endure our misunderstandings.

One day I came home from work and found Pina crying in her room. When I asked her what had happened, she said she had quarreled with my father. Her confession infuriated me, but in the hope of calming the tension, I rented an apartment the following day so we could live on our own. However, I was still angry with Pina and told her that since she could not get along with my people, I was never taking her back to see them.

This last straw damaged our relationship significantly. I took the baby to see my folks every Sunday, leaving Pina home alone. Of course, she was not happy with this arrangement and tried to sabotage my routine. As a result of this ongoing crisis, we had serious quarrels.

One particular Sunday, in a last-ditch attempt to stop me from taking Pino out, she succeeded in making me extremely angry. I let go with a torrent of invectives. "Stop forcing me to choose between you and my family. If things are not to your liking, let's just get a divorce. But either way I will still keep taking my son to visit my family. I'm his father, and I have a right to take him with me once a week wherever I choose—and no one in the world, including you, has a right to tell me or make me do otherwise."

Chapter 21

From that night on, I slept on the living room sofa, as Pina and I had stopped talking to each other. One morning, a few days later, I told her to call a lawyer and start the divorce proceedings. She never made that call, but we went on in that hostile manner for some time—ignoring each other like strangers with opposite agendas—yet living under the same roof.

During those awful days I searched my brain for an answer—did I or did I not want a divorce? Ultimately, I realized that despite all the hostility between us, I still loved Pina, and the thought of losing her was too much to bear. Plus, there was Pino to consider. He figured very prominently in our idea of what constituted a family and what life was all about.

The mere idea of seeing Pino grow up separated from me sent shivers down my spine. I thought for a moment how important it had been for me to grow up around my parents, and how painful it was now to see my sick father making his way through the last days of his life. Would it be fair for a child we purposely brought into this world to grow up deprived of his father's continuous care, support and love?

Did Pina and I have the right, simply out of selfishness, pride, and stubbornness, to abandon our child into the hands of a single parent—or were we obligated by love and duty to allow him the emotional security of a two-parent household? Perhaps it was time Pina and I set aside our pride, grew up, and got our act together. It was time we resolved our personal differences and started living for the sake of those we loved.

I made an effort to understand the real nature of our problems—and how best to resolve them. Neither of us could be right or wrong all the time, I thought. Anyway, a healthy relationship is built on "give" and "take" rather than on "right" or "wrong." The more I thought the more I came to the same conclusion—that in the long run, avoiding our problems and getting a divorce would be an admission of failure, with the likelihood of repeating our mistakes over and over again. I finally concluded I did not want a divorce.

In the meantime—maybe out of false pride—I found it difficult to take the first step toward reconciliation by telling Pina what I thought. And so we went on, leading a meaningless existence mingled with the bitterness of disappointment and sorrow.

Approximately two weeks later, Pina was unusually nervous when I returned from work. She waited a while, and then said she wanted to talk to me. I sat down across from her and asked her what she wanted.

Without looking at me, she said, "There's no way I can go on living like this."

In hearing those words my heart started beating faster. Then I tried to calm myself and collect my thoughts. I said, "Pina, I know my behavior indicates to the contrary, and I'm a failure at showing you the kind of affection you deserve, but I still love you—probably more than ever." After a moment of silence and a glance in her direction, I continued in a more contrite tone. "Don't leave me, Pina. If not for me, at least for our son."

We looked at each other in the eyes and burst into tears. We then hugged each other with all our might, remaining locked in an embrace for a long while. Then, as if by common agreement and without uttering a word, we proceeded to the bedroom and made the most passionate love of our married lives—so ecstatic were we at being back in each other's arms.

The following day, I decided not to go to work. After getting out of bed, Pina asked me if I was hungry. I confessed that after all the lovemaking of the previous night, I was as famished as a wolf and needed to get my strength back. After a wonderful breakfast, I told her how much I loved and appreciated her. She told me how much she loved me, as well, and that despite all the harsh words and misunderstandings we had been through, she would do anything to save our marriage and keep the family together.

I suggested we start by pinpointing the true nature of our problems and resolve them as best we could. She confessed she feared being

Chapter 21

criticized when she was around my folks. I assured her she would no longer have to see them—thus avoiding any further feelings of friction. Next thing on her list of grievances was that I worked too much and spent too much of my leisure time with my family—creating a detachment from her and Pino that was not compatible with her idea of a good marriage. In the future she wanted me to spend more time with her and our little one and remember they too were a part of my life.

I assured her I loved them both too much to ever dream of forgetting them. "From now on, I promise, I will try to spend as much time as I can at home and with you and Pino. But you have to understand that in order to cover all the household expenses, I have to work two jobs."

Pina smiled back.

"But you must understand and respect the closeness and love that exists between me and my family—and never try to interfere," I said. "This is the time for me to show them my love and devotion. Once they're gone, it will be too late, and I would never be able to forgive myself—or you, if I didn't do that." I took her hands in mine. "Do you understand what I'm trying to say?"

"Yes," She replied, barely audible. She sighed. "I will make a great effort to never again interfere with your relationship with your folks." Then she pleaded with me one more time to promise never to forget her or our child.

I reassured her that nothing in the world would ever make me forget either of them.

And so with these promises made, we moved toward a new future, which, thanks to our new honesty, common sense, and strong communication, looked so much brighter than our past.

In the meanwhile, Gioacchino, with the help of some friends, had been in touch with an Italian girl. He traveled to Italy to meet her with the understanding that if they liked each other, they would get married. He left on his trip in April, 1973. It took only a couple of weeks for him to call and announce the date of his wedding.

For obvious reasons, neither my father nor mother could attend the ceremony. Ignazio, seventeen at the time, was still too young. That left it to me to represent the family at Gioacchino's wedding in Italy. I broke the news to Pina that I had to go to Italy for a week. She immediately reminded me that given our financial state, there was no way we could handle the expense.

Looking straight into her eyes, I said, "I would never allow him to get married alone in a faraway place—as if no one cared about him. It is my duty and I will go."

"But we don't even have the necessary things for the house yet," Pina said, glancing around our modest rented home. I waved my hand at her. "It would be better if you said nothing at all right now. No one is more painfully aware of the conditions under which we live, but nothing and no one is going to keep me from representing our family at my brother's wedding. There is no gift he would appreciate more—and it's one he's earned from me a hundred times over."

When Pina realized how determined I was, she packed my suitcases in silent acceptance.

The day before I left for Italy, my father told me he had decided to sell the remainder of our property in Ribera, the family house and a plot of land he had entrusted to his brother Lillo. For that reason, he wanted me to go to Ribera after the wedding and ask his brother if he was interested in buying our property.

"How much do you want for the land?" I asked.

"Ten million lire," he said. At the time, this was the approximate equivalent of eleven thousand U.S dollars.

"Papa, the land is worth more than that."

"I know it," he answered. "If he is not interested in buying it, try to sell it to somebody else."

The next day I left for Italy. My brother, his future wife Rosa, and Rosa's mother were waiting for me at the airport. On the following morning, to my surprise, Zio *(uncle)* Lillo, Zia *(aunt)* Lina, and their son Antonio all arrived from Ribera to attend the wedding ceremony. After a beautiful wedding feast, I joined my uncle and family on a plane to Palermo, rented a car and drove on to Ribera where I visited with my in-laws, who had moved back to Cattolica Eraclea from Montreal.

During my short stay in Ribera, I informed Zio Lillo of my father's precarious state of health and of his intention to sell the property he had entrusted to him, relating to him what my father told me. Zio Lillo said he was interested in the purchase, but he didn't have the cash on hand. If we were willing to delay the sale, it would give him time to sell one of his two houses. However, he was only willing to pay eight million lire.

I told him I could not speak for my father on the price, and that as long as he remained alive, the final answer was up to him. Then I made it clear to him that according to my sources, the market value for the property was between eighteen and twenty million lire, almost double what my father was asking.

"You have the wrong information," Zio Lillo said. "The land is not worth that much money."

"When I get back to the States," I said, "I will tell my father everything you said, including the price you are willing to pay. We'll let you know."

When I returned to Waterbury, I told my father the price his brother was willing to pay for the property. I was expecting him to be angry—and he was. He asked me to write to Zio Lillo immediately and tell him that if the price we asked was not to his liking, we would simply sell the property to someone else. To me, he confided that if his brother found our price too stiff, knowing full well the property was worth a lot more, it meant his brother was an unscrupulous and inveterate egotist who was only looking out for himself, and would show and prove that his brother did not care about the conditions under which we were living. This was a big blow, as he had never expected anything like this from his brother.

Exhausted as he was, my father needed to express his feelings to me. "If your Zio Lillo's heart were in the right place, he would not have acted in that way, since he is perfectly aware of the dire financial straits we're in." My father was now terminally ill with cancer, had been out of work for a long time, and completely dependent on his children.

A few weeks later we received a letter from my uncle saying he was interested in buying the property, provided we wait until he sold one of his houses so he could pay us.

Now, didn't this mean he was willing to accept our conditions? Only time would tell. We began a long wait.

Meanwhile, my father's health steadily deteriorated. He endured excruciating pain throughout his body and was constantly on painkillers, which attenuated the discomfort somewhat.

The entire family suffered a great deal, mostly because there was nothing we could do about his pain or his physical deterioration. Once again, I couldn't help wondering how God, provided He existed, could allow such personal calamities to afflict the creatures He brought into being.

I continued to ponder the reason for existence in this world, where most of the time the extent of our suffering is disproportionate to our ephemeral delights.

I was so discouraged during this period that I became vulnerable to the same ups and downs I experienced during my student days. Now, as then, I had no incentive to go on living what seemed to be a harsh and meaningless existence. I no longer felt driven by the desire to accomplish anything and doubted my ability to carry out even the simplest of tasks. Nature itself, I was convinced, had conspired against me and my family. The dream of acquiring a sound economic position had vanished into thin air, and I had replaced my battle for success with one for pure survival. I felt like a mouse in a cage, hopeless and without any chance of escape—living in fear the cage itself would devour me. I was preoccupied

Chapter 21

with thinking it was better to die and put an end to it all.

The thing that gave me the drive to get up in the morning and to work seven days a week—from early morning till evening—was the knowledge that I was doing it all for the sake of my wife, my son, and the other members of my family who desperately needed my help.

Relief for me came in the company of my little son, Pino, who was growing up and becoming increasingly more handsome and delightful—never failing to bring joy into our otherwise downcast hearts. There was bittersweet gratification as well in seeing my father every evening when I came home from work and being able to talk to him about the day's events.

Around the end of 1973, we purchased a lot on which to build a triplex, which would allow one unit for Pina, Pino, and me; a second for Gioacchino and his wife, who were now living in Waterbury; and one for my father, mother, and Ignazio. After securing a loan from a local bank, we started construction.

CHAPTER 22
Father's Death and Business Disaster

On Christmas Day of 1973, at my parents' constant urging, I asked Pina if she wanted to join the whole family in celebrating the holiday. She replied she would be happy to do so. After getting our little Pino ready, we went to my parents' home. This was to be a most important and auspicious occasion since, following the rather unfortunate misunderstandings of the recent past, we were all finally able to sit together at the table, united as a family, and enjoy the fruits of harmony and love for which our hearts yearned.

Soon after the holidays, Pina and I, along with Gioacchino and Rosa, enrolled in a night school course to improve our English. One evening, the manager of a newly opened bank came to give a talk at the school. The address turned out to be extremely interesting, and even later on in my life, I still found it useful. The topic dealt with the criteria bank managers used in making decisions on whether to grant a loan.

When a bank considers a loan application, the first thing the manager does is appraise the client's character and personal abilities. Most of the time, the loan is granted according to the degree of trust an applicant is able to instill in the interviewer. Thus, according to the guest speaker, whenever someone looks for a bank loan, it is important to be prepared to answer every question with assurance and steadfastness—and to explain clearly the reason for the loan, as well as the terms under which it will be paid. One's pledge to comply with the payments, needless to say, is the most important part of the transaction.

Chapter 22

I will always remember the bank manager's talk as one of the most important lessons in my life—the simple principles he enumerated taught me how to face similar situations in the future. Now I felt confident about what to say to a bank manager and how to successfully overcome the stumbling blocks that occasionally came my way in dealing with banks.

A few months after this episode, the idea of importing foodstuffs from Italy and selling them to the various food markets in and around Waterbury occurred to me as a good idea. I thought that if I could secure a small loan and start importing the goods on a small scale, I could use the profits to expand my business. I decided to go see the bank manager who had come to our school and tell him about my plans. After listening carefully to my proposal, he agreed my idea had merit and wanted to know how much I needed. I said $5,000.00 would be enough. When he asked how soon I could start importing the goods, I told him as soon as I had the money. That's when he told me I could have the money right away—as soon as I filled out an application and opened an account with the bank.

After spending the next half-hour being interviewed for the loan, I left the bank with $5,000.00 deposited in my new account. I was euphoric beyond words. Having gone to see the bank manager for advice and information, I never dreamed I would come away with a loan—it had been so simple. I ran home, bursting to share the good news.

The days following were filled with joy and optimism. After getting a list of prospective Italian export companies from the Italian Consulate, Pina and I began writing letters. Reaction to our inquiries was discouraging. We were generally advised that in order to get good discounts we had to place large orders, which would have to be paid for in advance. The $5,000.00 loan did not even cover the first order. That's when it dawned on me that I simply could not get started in the import business without substantial funding.

Despite this first stumbling block, I refused to give up. I knew

Montreal had many Italian food manufacturers, so I decided to go there in the hope of securing a few contracts—expecting a more favorable treatment, since the distance between Waterbury and Montreal was shorter.

In Montreal, I went to see Leonardo Cacciatore, my friend from Winnipeg who had moved to Montreal after marrying Pina's cousin. Thanks to his help, I was able to make contact with several firms, but the same rules applied here as in Italy. The companies were only interested in large orders and payment in advance. Obviously, I was terribly disappointed.

Leonardo approached me with the idea of forming a company with him to import clothing from Italy to be sold in Canada. He assured me that only a relatively small amount of capital was required to start out. Of course, I told him I had no experience in the clothing business and considered it risky to invest in an enterprise about which I knew nothing. He dismissed my concerns, telling me he had run a clothing store for about two years. I told him I would have to consult with my family before giving a response. So I returned to Waterbury and recounted the whole Montreal outcome to the family, admitting the best course of action would be to forget the idea of importing food.

I presented Leonardo Cacciatore's proposal about importing clothing from Italy. We all agreed that none of us had experience in that industry, and we would have to depend solely on my cousin's expertise to get us through the initial phase of doing business. Ultimately, we agreed that as much as we liked the idea, we would have to wait, as we had no desire to incur another loan. I called Leonardo and told him how we felt—and that as soon as we could accumulate enough money to get started, we would want to move forward with him. He understood and said that since he did not have start-up capital either, he was willing to wait until we were ready.

I had great doubts about the feasibility of our new enterprise—coupled with dread, fear and massive confusion. But I could not understand why I felt as I did. After a while, I consciously suppressed

Chapter 22

the negative feelings, trying to convince myself my doubts were unfounded and that everything was going to be all right.

Time was flying. It was the beginning of 1974 and construction work on our new house was proceeding relatively well, if a bit too slow due to the fact Gioacchino and I were doing a lot of the work to save on costs. We figured, in any case, that we would be through by the end of May. My father's health was still bad; as if to compensate for his grandfather's decline, my son was growing up healthy and beautiful.

One day we received a letter from Zio Lillo and Zia Lina, informing us they had finally sold their house in Ribera and were ready to close the deal on our property. They were asking for power of attorney so they could have the deed drawn up and ultimately send us the money. Instinctively, I advised my parents not to sign over any power of attorney. Instead, we would demand they draw up a contract and send it to us to be signed before a notary public, after which it would go back to Italy for registration.

Zio Lillo and Zia Lina were disappointed by our response and reiterated their contention that the fair value of the property was only eight million lire, not ten—yet they were willing to make a sacrifice on our behalf and raise their offer to nine. Furthermore, if we did not agree, I (who they considered the head of the household now) could go to Ribera and try to sell it for a better price.

This letter upset us all enormously. It was clear they had requested power of attorney in order to draw up a deed to their specifications and pay us whatever amount they chose in order to purchase the property—automatically depriving us of any legal recourse in the process. Their deceitful behavior left us cold for two reasons. First, when they wrote us after my return from Italy and specified that after the sale of their house they would close the deal with us, it was logical to assume they had accepted our proposal without further reservations. Second, they bided their time, probably thinking that if we contested their price, the Italian laws then in force would have favored them—and with the distance between us, we would ultimately cave to their demands.

But this letter had the opposite effect. Instead of discouraging us, it galvanized our family unit. We finally accepted the obvious—these people were acting in their own self-interest and completely dismissive of the fact that for many years they had enjoyed the benefits of the property without ever paying us one lira in rent. On top of that, they were not even appreciative of the fact that we were willing to sell the property to them at half the market value.

I could not understand what made them so mercenary and why they chose to take advantage of us now—when in the past we had been so close and fond of one another. How could they show such lack of compassion, knowing my father's condition and that he had not worked a day in three and-a-half years?

To make sure I was not being unfair, I called a friend in Ribera to ask his opinion on the land's fair market value. He made some inquiries and called me back. "Not only is the land worth twenty million lire, but I have a client who wants to buy it immediately, and if you can wait a while longer, we can probably get you even more. It's up to you, of course."

I related the news to my mother and brothers, making sure my father got no wind of it, as it undoubtedly would have caused him distress. "The best course of action at this point is for me to go to Ribera and confront Zio *(uncle)* Lillo and Zia *(aunt)* Lina face-to-face. If they want the land, they'll have to pay fair market value like anyone else. They showed no compassion for us, and we can't afford to show compassion for them." A few days later I left for Italy.

On my way to Ribera, I stopped off in Catania, where my wife's aunt lived. I thought it wise to consult with her attorney son-in-law to determine a solution in case I could not reach an agreement with my uncle and aunt. Then, I preceded to Cattolica Eraclea to see my in-laws, my sister-in-law Paola, and her fiancé, Angelo.

The following day, accompanied by Angelo, I arrived in Ribera and went directly to my uncle's house. He and my aunt were very surprised to see me, to say the least. Zia *(aunt)* Lina actually clutched her heart

Chapter 22

in shock as the blood drained from her face. Zio *(uncle)* Lillo looked equally alarmed. It took two weeks of heated discussions, but with the help of Angelo, we made a verbal agreement in the amount of fifteen million lire—after which we sent instructions to the notary to prepare the necessary documentation to finalize the sale.

While I was going through this process, Pina phoned me saying that my father's condition was getting worse, and he had to be taken to the hospital. A strange foreboding took hold of me. "Pina," I said. "See if the doctors can keep him alive for just a few more days. I need to talk with him one last time." That night I was unable to sleep, convinced there was very little time left to see my father.

On the next morning, May 9, I spoke with my in-laws about giving my mother-in-law power of attorney to close the sale on my behalf. I would be leaving for the United States the following day. That night, at 3:15 a.m. the phone rang. I felt certain it was Pina calling. My mother-in-law picked up the phone before me, and from the expression on her face, I knew what had happened. She passed the receiver to me, saying that it was Pina on the line.

Pina was sobbing as I took the receiver. "The doctors did what they could to keep him alive, but it was all in vain. At nine o'clock last night, he passed away and committed his soul to God."

Approximately half an hour later, accompanied by Paola and Angelo, I left for the airport to catch the Palermo-Rome-New York flight. Later in the evening, I arrived home in Waterbury. My cousins Maria and Teresa, as well as Teresa's husband, had come down from Montreal for the funeral. The next morning, I went to the funeral home. When I saw my father inside the casket, I felt numb, finding it impossible to even cry.

Looking at him, I noticed deep marks of suffering etched across his face. I got down on my knees in front of the coffin and spoke with him mentally, asking him to forgive me for having been away during the last days of his life and not being able to offer him comfort and assistance when he most needed it. I told him that if I had known,

Our house at 62 Ball Farm Road, Oakville, Conn. Near Waterbury.

Pino in front of our fireplace on Christmas. Oakville, Conn. 1974.

I would have never left his bedside. "I want to thank you for all the sacrifices you endured on behalf of your family, the care you bestowed on us, and the inspiration of your incomparable example. Above all, I thank you for the great love you bore all of us. Please understand we loved you in equal measure." I stopped for a moment to collect my thoughts before continuing. "Please don't ever forsake me. Please love and protect me now as you did when you were alive. I need you now and always will." At that moment, as if a big lump had come loose from my throat, I was able to weep out my grief.

Two days later, two more cousins, Leonardo Cacciatore and Nicola Russo, came in from Montreal to attend the funeral. After my father was laid to rest and our relatives left town, we found ourselves grieving alone and coping as well as we could. It was particularly difficult for me to accept the cruel reality of fate. I was convinced I would never be able to overcome my emotional difficulties and would ultimately succumb to the depths of such despair.

Around the middle of June we finally ended our work on the house and moved in. What should have been a joyous occasion turned out to be a sad and painful one. We were thinking of our father and wondered what it would have been like to share this moment with him.

Meanwhile, Gioacchino and I had acquired our American citizenship, making us feel like an integral part of this great country. It was already autumn, and my cousin Leonardo phoned me from Montreal to see if I was ready to begin our business enterprise. I talked things over with Gioacchino and Ignazio, and we agreed to move ahead, despite the heightened state of confusion and uncertainty I felt deep in my heart.

There were many Italian shops in Montreal at that time, so Leonardo and I examined the possibilities for success in Winnipeg, arriving at the conclusion that an Italian clothing shop would net us a fortune. Accordingly, we rented a store and then left for Italy to purchase the goods. Upon my return from Italy, Pina and I rented out our apartment in Oakville to help pay the monthly mortgage and then with our son Pino, we moved to Winnipeg. After about one month of intensive work, we opened for business. Pina and I stayed in Winnipeg to run the store, and Leonardo returned to Montreal.

As the days went by, I noticed the local people showed little interest in our products. As a result, we neither sold nor earned anything. With the passage of time, this embarrassing predicament grew worse. It got to the point where Pina and I could no longer take a paycheck and we could not afford to buy groceries. To make ends meet, we ended up getting a job cleaning offices at night. Thus, in the daytime we had to mind the store, and at night we had to work as office cleaners in order to survive.

It was obvious we could not keep going on that way, and that our clothing store would not even pay the electrical bill and the rent. I called Leonardo to explain that it might be best to shut down the operation. He came to Winnipeg, and saw for himself that I was right. We promoted a big going-out-of-business sale, disposing of whatever we could, and then packed the remainder to ship to Montreal, where we hoped to sell it and make up for some of our losses.

And so ended with disastrous results our foray into the world of business. In six months' time my family suffered losses amounting to $22,500.00 which represented all the savings we had been able to accumulate, plus part of the profits from the sale of our property in Ribera.

As if we weren't depressed enough, we were forced to suffer the criticism of some friends and family members who found the whole idea of opening a business in Winnipeg "foolhardy and ridiculous." Pina and I arrived in Montreal, penniless and disillusioned.

CHAPTER 23
First Encounter with a Clairvoyant

After we arrived in Montreal, we stayed with Leonardo for a few days. During that time, we tried to sell all we could of the remaining stock and split between us what was left. Then we moved in with my cousin Maria and her family. While we were staying there, I was determined to understand the precise cause of our miserable failure, so I analyzed in detail as objectively as I could the facts of our experience in Winnipeg, which cost my family $22,500.00—all our savings and most of the money from the sale of the land to Zio *(uncle)* Lillo in Ribera. After careful study, it became clear the failure of the business and our financial fiasco was due to our commercial incompetence and ignorance of the clothing industry.

Most of the goods we bought in Italy were already out of fashion, and we wouldn't have been able to give them away. I realized I should never have gone into a business about which I knew nothing.

I blamed myself for the financial disaster I had brought upon my family, and I was so angry at myself and so hurt by what I'd done that at times I couldn't decide whether to scream with all the force I had within me or hit my head against a concrete wall. Everything happened so fast I had a hard time believing the tragic reality of what I'd done.

Frequent shudders of fear tormented me—something I had never faced before, at least to that degree. This new sensation had a thoroughly paralyzing effect on me: I could no longer rouse myself into facing responsibilities and I grew increasingly insecure and unable to function. This was one of the darkest times of my life.

Pina, my mother, my brothers, and my cousin Maria all advised me to accept the reality of the situation, to forget what had happened and to look forward to the future. I could only ask them what future they were talking about, since I was convinced I had already destroyed my future.

"You must take positive action," they insisted.

"That's easier said than done," I replied.

A few days went by, and in an attempt to find my way through this, I asked myself the following:

- **What can I do to recuperate the lost money?**
- **What am I going to do next?**
- **Where am I going to live?**
- **Should I go back to Waterbury?**
- **Should I stay in Montreal?**
- **How will I know which choices will turn out to be the right ones, so I don't end up involved in another disaster?**

Not being able to find the answers to these questions combined with the overwhelming fear of making a wrong decision left me in a state of total confusion.

One night as I lay in bed, restless and wracked with mental turmoil, my mother's healing experience came to mind. I instinctively said to myself:

My God, even if I do not understand who You are, where You are, and how You work, I am sure that at this very moment You know the problems I face. I pray for You to guide me toward the right decision for me and my family, and toward a more peaceful and more secure future.

As I repeated this prayer, I began to calm down. Then, from the deepest place in my heart, as though a voice were talking to me, I perceived the following:

Paolo, in order to get out of the pit you got into, and to find

peace of mind, you need to recover the money you lost. Working as a simple laborer will take too much time—years, in fact. The only way to recover that money fairly quickly and to fulfill your life long desire, is to go into business once again. The business you need to go into is the one that was your original goal when you arrived in the U.S.—asphalt paving. The right place for you to do that is Montreal.

But before you make any business plans, you must spend a minimum of two years working for a paving company. During that period you will come to terms with your emotions; you will learn the basic mechanics of the trade; you will become familiar with the working environment of the area; you will get to know the available work force; you will save some money to start your operation; and finally, if you find yourself in desperate need of help, your brother Gioacchino will be able to join you at any time, considering he will be only 350 miles away—six and-a-half hours by car.

As I considered the above, the fear and uncertainty pervading my mind and my heart vanished. In its place was a sense of peace and hope for the future—a feeling I thought I would never again experience. Then I fell into a calm sleep.

I woke up the next morning feeling relaxed, rested, and at peace with myself. I was more animated than I had been in a long while, with a strong desire to fight back and start all over again. After Pina got up, I shared my perceptions with her. She thought for a moment. "Winters in Montreal are worse than they are in Waterbury, but I still prefer Montreal. I have a feeling that if we're careful, this is where we'll find what we've been looking for." We decided to stay in Montreal and give it a try.

The evening of that same day, we told my cousins Maria and Pasquale of our decision and of our desire to find work in Montreal. They were enthusiastic. Pasquale told me the company where he worked did plenty of asphalt jobs and was hiring new workers for a project slated to start the first part of July in James Bay, which was located in the north of Quebec Province, approximately a thousand miles from Montreal.

Pasquale said the crews worked seven days a week there and were guaranteed a minimum of ten hours a day. A job like that offered far more earning potential than any in Montreal. Since it was now Friday night and the office would be closed the following day, he volunteered to take me to his company's employment office at six o'clock Monday morning and introduce me to the hiring manager, who would be able to tell me whether or not work was available for me.

I thanked Pasquale and assured him I would be happy to go with him on Monday.

The next evening, Pina, Pino, and I had supper with two of Pina's cousins—Pietro and Joe Salvo—and their respective families. They mentioned they owned a construction company that was installing sewer and water systems. I told them I had done that kind of work in the United States and had acquired a fair amount of experience. Pietro was ready to hire me on the spot, but I told him about my interest in working for an asphalt-paving company and my plans for the future. He told me that if I should ever need a job, all I had to do was ask him, and he would be very glad to help me out.

Just as he had promised, Pasquale picked me up on Monday and introduced me to the person in charge of hiring at the company where he worked. I told him I'd like to work in James Bay. Without giving me any kind of response, the man sized me up from head to foot, paying particular attention to my hands, and then asked me if I had ever worked with asphalt before. I replied I had about three years' experience in that kind of work. After looking at my hands once more, as if scrutinizing them, he grimaced and suggested that I stay in the waiting room if I liked, and he would let me know if he had anything available later in the morning. Then he headed for his office and completely ignored me.

Through the window, I saw the laborers gradually going off to work, whereas I was left waiting. Around nine o'clock, the man came back into the waiting room and told me there was nothing available that day.

"Will there be anything tomorrow?" I asked hopefully.

"I can't say right now, but if you like, you can come back tomorrow and take your chances."

Disappointed, I returned home, but agreed to try again the next day.

The following morning, I went back as I said I would. After the crews had gone to work, the hiring manager came out and told me exactly the same thing as he had the day before: Nothing was available the rest of the day.

Once again, I asked if he had anything for the next day. His answer was, "Maybe. Try again in the morning."

For the second day in a row I went home disappointed and worried.

The next morning I returned for the third time. Again, after all the crews had gone to work, the hiring manager came out and told me nothing was available for me, but I might try again the next day.

In hearing those words, I looked him straight in the eye and demanded, "What the hell kind of man are you? If you don't have any work for me or if you just don't want to hire me, say so. I could be looking for work elsewhere. But if your major concern is whether or not I can do the job, try me for a week. If I don't meet your expectations, don't pay me."

The man was shocked by this outburst from someone he clearly considered an underling. He scrutinized me again from head to toe, shaking his head. Then, he looked me straight in the face and told me to wait a moment while he went back to his office. A few minutes later, he came back with a safety helmet and told me to board a particular truck loaded with asphalt that would take me to work.

I tried to apologize for the way I had acted, but with a wave of his hand he rendered me silent and signaled me to get in the truck. That was the bizarre way I got the job. Later that evening I told Pasquale what had happened, and he was shocked. "The man is impossible. Everyone who works with him lives in fear of offending him. No one who knows him would have the guts to talk to him like that." He smiled and shook his head in wonderment.

A few days later, Pina found a job in a factory that made leather jackets. Once again we were able to settle down and start earning income. When I got my wages on the following Friday, we used the money to rent a basement apartment in a triplex that consisted of two very small rooms: a bedroom, a kitchen-sitting-dining-room combination, and an extremely modest bathroom. We brought in all the boxes full of clothes we couldn't sell and, for lack of space, stored them in the bedroom. Then, we bought a mattress and bed frame that we managed to squeeze between the boxes. After weeks of wandering from place to place, we were finally able to sleep in our own place again.

On Sunday morning, Maria and Pasquale came over and observed that besides the bed, we had no furniture, not even a fridge.

"As long we don't have the money to purchase one, we will just have to buy our food on a daily basis," I said.

They volunteered the use of their refrigerator for our perishables and suggested we cook and eat at their house in the evening. We accepted their offer, for the time being.

That same afternoon, while Pina, Pino, and I rested on the bed, Pina confessed that since marrying me she no longer attended Holy Mass, and that she missed it. She wondered if I had attended church regularly before we met. Until that moment, we had never spoken about religion, and I found her sudden interest in the subject surprising. I explained that when I was in Ribera, I attended services regularly on Sundays. But after leaving there I had only gone to church on special occasions, like weddings, baptisms, and funerals. She wanted to know why, and I told her that the Church's guiding principles where

Chapter 23

filled with mystery and dogma making it impossible to understand their teachings. On top of that, I had the impression that the church purposely kept people in total and absurd ignorance.

Another reason was due to the conduct and the lifestyle of the clergy in general. Most of the priests I had known—with the exception of Padre Territo from Ribera—did not practice what they preached and created a dichotomy between their wolfish instincts and the image they tried to project as shepherds of God's flock. Most of the priests in that part of the world led an active political life and, on the whole, a prosperous and comfortable existence compared to the average people in town. Also, I felt the majority of priests demonstrated a far greater attachment to material considerations than to spiritual ones. And in matters of morality, faith, purity, and chastity, all too many men of the cloth took advantage of their special status to prey on the weaker, more naive women of their congregations.

I told Pina I had never understood, and consequently could not accept, the Church's doctrine and spiritual messages. Then I went on to relate my childhood experiences with the nuns and the town priests. Accordingly, I told her, I recognized and respected the clergy simply as fellow human beings independent of their function or self-proclaimed mission as spiritual leaders of the community. I found attending church a bore, a waste of time, and nothing more than a formality. To me, it was completely devoid of deep spiritual significance. In spite of my feelings about the clergy, however, deep in my heart I always had a great desire to understand what God was about—but I had never found anyone who could help me in my quest for religious enlightenment.

I had read the New Testament in the hope of finding help and comfort in the message of Jesus Christ. But I concluded that the Sacred Scriptures were on a par with children's fairy tales. I was particularly convinced it was impossible to apply Jusus' doctrines in dealing with some of our fellow human beings, especially when it came to forgiveness.

Looking at the arrogance and egoism of so many people, I couldn't help thinking that the Old Testament passage ***"OCCHIO PER OCCHIO E DENTE PER DENTE"*** (*"An eye for an eye and a tooth for a tooth"*)—is more realistic and effective in the course of daily life than the passive principles of Jesus. The only way to fight strength was through strength, and arrogance through arrogance. If someone slaps you in the face, you don't "turn the other cheek." You give him back what he gave you, and more. Nothing is more effective in dealing with people who hurt you than to hurt them right back—then they'll think twice before doing it again. I firmly believed that forgiving "those who trespass against us" would only be interpreted as a sign of weakness, encouraging evildoers to intensify their actions. As for the miracles attributed to Jesus, they simply left me cold and confused, engendering in my mind serious questions about their basis in fact. I doubted that such feats could ever be performed by anyone, regardless of how much faith they had.

"Do you believe such miracles can happen?" I asked Pina. Then I stopped talking and tried to ponder what I had just said. A strange perception passed through my mind. I could not explain to myself why, on the one hand, reason made me think and believe in everything I had just said, and on the other, like most other people, I instinctively invoked God's name and protection whenever the necessity arose. I wondered how such a paradox could exist in both my thoughts and actions. How could this be explained?

I told Pina about my mother's illness and eventual cure in Sicily that was brought about through the miraculous intervention of the little old healer. Pina listened in amazement. After I finished, Pina took my hand in hers. "I had no idea you ever thought about spiritual concepts," she said.

I smiled.

"Really. I thought the only thing you ever thought about was work."

We dropped it at that.

One evening a few days later, over dinner at the home of Maria

Chapter 23

and Pasquale, we talked about my financial failure and what might be at the root of it. Maria was convinced someone had given me *"IL MOLOCCHIO" ("The evil eye").* I burst into laughter, asking her if she truly believed in such nonsense. "It's nothing to laugh at," she replied, her eyes wide. "I know such curses take place, and it's unwise to underestimate their power."

Maria told me she knew a ninety-eight year-old French Canadian clairvoyant who would probably be able to tell me whether my problems were due to coincidence or to the evil eye. Prodded by Maria's urging, I gave in to curiosity and agreed to meet the old woman. Maria promised to find the woman's phone number and to contact her on my behalf.

The following evening, Maria told me she had booked me an appointment for nine o'clock that Saturday morning. I asked Pina if she wanted to accompany me, and she laughed. "You know I don't believe in such rubbish. The whole idea is a waste of time. But if you feel you have to go, by all means, go." She shook her head in disbelief. "It will be interesting," I said. "We can find out if there are people who really can foretell the future or if it's just nonsense." Pina shrugged, then looked me in the eyes and said, "Okay, if this is what you want, I will come."

On Saturday morning, Pina, my cousins, and I went to see the old woman. She greeted us courteously and invited us to sit in the living room. Then, she asked who wanted to have the first reading. Pina and my cousins looked at me, so I followed the petite clairvoyant into the next room.

Considering her age, she moved with vitality and ease. Her gentle, placid face radiated joy and peace, and her friendly smile immediately put me at ease, making me feel as though I had always known her.

The small room was simply furnished with a modest table and two chairs, where we sat across from each other. She looked into my eyes and asked, "Why did you want to see me, and what do you want to find out?"

I smiled and shrugged. "I don't exactly know, but I'm curious to hear what you might have to tell me."

She opened a drawer in the table, out of which she drew a large deck of strange-looking cards, the likes of which I had never seen before. Then she asked me to shuffle them, cut the deck, and hand them over to her.

After I did that, she laid the cards down face-up, placing them according to a pre-arranged order. After carefully examining them, she lowered her head and, deeply absorbed in thought, spoke without looking at me. "You have recently lost your father," she said. She described the particular details of his illness and suffering, and the grief I had gone through in not being able to assist him during the last few days of his life. She even explained the problems we had with my uncle.

Then, she went on to speak about my efforts to go into business, describing again, in minute detail, the events that had taken place. She talked about the fiasco with the clothing shop in Winnipeg, explaining why and how it had occurred.

The woman went on to describe my character, and Pina's as well. She concentrated on our marital relationship, describing the fiery arguments that often went on, the deep love that comprised the core of our strong bond, and the respect we bore each other.

She told me to put out of my mind the notion that anyone wanted to harm me, either through the evil eye or through any other form or shape of sorcery. She explained that all my problems and failures were simply due to the complex nature of my personality and character, and my frequent doubts kept me from making the right decisions at crucial times. "You must stop worrying about making mistakes," she said. "It is this fear that is the major cause of your problems."

Then she looked up at me and smiled warmly. "The things I have told you are no cause for alarm. You are endowed with uncommon gifts and abilities, and you'll be able to easily overcome most problems."

"In time," she continued, "you will learn about the mechanisms of life, and how its seemingly unrelated elements are interconnected and working together. After that, your life will undergo enormous changes, and you will successfully overcome whatever difficulties lay ahead. You will be able to determine the course of your future at will." Again, she smiled. "Now, you must stop worrying about the negativities of the past and concentrate instead on the present, with an eye toward the future. You will soon be presented with an opportunity to change jobs, which you must do."

She leaned back. "By so doing," she said, "not only will you have the chance to earn more money that you desperately need at this particular time in your life, but you will also have an experience that will be of enormous help to you for the rest of your life. You need to simply act with greater determination, resolution, and assurance than you have in the past, and when faced with options, you need to learn how to make the right decision."

"That's more easily said than done," I said. "How can I know in the present that the decision I'm making is the right one for the future?"

"If you pay close attention, you will always know it."

"It's impossible to know beforehand which is the right decision and the right thing to do."

She shook her head. "You are wrong. It is, in fact, easier than you think. You'll see."

Once again, I was about to tell her she was wrong, there was no way in the world we could be sure the decisions we make are the right ones, but she stopped me by slightly raising the calm tone of her voice and commanding my silence with a wave of her hand. "When the time comes, pay close attention to your instinct, and you will know the right course of action to follow." She took a deep breath. "You have nothing for which to envy anyone, since you are endowed with the ability to do anything you want to do, as long you put your mind to it." She looked straight at me. "Now, do you have any other questions?"

"Yes," I replied. "How do you know all these things about me without knowing me at all?"

"Through God's divine will." She gave me her blessing and her permission to leave.

I thanked her, assuring her I would never forget her. When I stood, she reminded me to quit my present job as soon the occasion presented itself, because that would mark the beginning of a new life for me.

Pina and then my cousins had a reading with the clairvoyant after me, and they were all astonished by what she told them.

After we returned home, the following questions regarding my reading with the clairvoyant stimulated my curiosity:

- **How could she know as much as she did about my private life?**
- **Was she endowed with supernatural powers?**
- **Was she superhuman?**
- **Was she a normal individual who through study and application had reached such a high degree of consciousness as to be able to penetrate into people's hearts and mind and see into their past and future?**

There had to be a logical explanation, so I asked myself:

- **Where could I find the explanation for her powers?**
- **To whom should I go to discover the truth?**

Once again I found myself confronted by an impenetrable wall, enveloped in a deep mystery. I could do nothing but keep alive the hope that someday, somehow, I would understand the facts behind the riddles.

Ultimately, the discoveries and explanations did come—not in the way I had expected, but slowly, one at a time.

CHAPTER 24
James Bay

Meanwhile, despite the difficulties of daily existence, Pina and I were gradually growing more relaxed. We continued to work, and even managed to put some money aside. At the rate we were going, we would soon have enough to buy a refrigerator, a stove, and a table with some chairs. Although we had many friends and relatives in Montreal, we didn't socialize—not because we didn't want to, but because we had none of the essentials for home entertainment.

The last Wednesday morning in June, my boss relayed that the James Bay project was ready to get moving and members of the asphalt-laying crew were to leave for the site on Saturday night. At home that evening, I gave Pina the news. She lowered her head and turned around with her back to me—not speaking a word. I hugged her from behind and then gently turned her around. Tears ran down her cheeks. "Time will fly," I said. "You'll see. And before long I'll be home, and we'll have enough money to dig ourselves out of this hole of poverty."

She continued listening in silence. Then, in a barely audible voice, as if afraid to speak her mind, she explained that she didn't want to stay in that basement apartment without the essentials for survival. Nor did she feel capable of going on foot to my cousin Maria's for meals, nor taking Pino to the baby-sitter. Still crying, she told me in an almost imperceptible voice that she was frightened at the thought of staying in Montreal by herself in those conditions. "Please don't go to James Bay and leave me and Pino here alone," she whispered.

A lump in my throat made it difficult for me to speak. With tears welling in my eyes, I hugged her tightly to make her realize I understood her concern and completely agreed with her. After a moment, I spoke in a shaky voice, almost stammering. "The right thing to do now is to stay close to each other. I promise to talk with my boss in the morning and ask him to mediate on my behalf with the general manager and convince him not to send me to James Bay."

Then we went to bed, but I couldn't sleep. I worried what I should say or, more importantly, what excuse I could invent to win my boss' compassion and support.

The wife of a friend of mine had recently gone through surgery for the removal of a fibroma, and I decided to tell my boss that Pina was affected by that tumor, that the doctor did not know yet what he was going to do, and that I needed to be near her. I thought and believed that this excuse was going to do the trick, and I was going to be able to save my job. For most of the night, I mentally repeated what I was going to say and how I was going to say it.

When I got to work the next morning, I called my boss aside and gave him the excuse I had made up during the night. He replied that he was very sorry about the whole matter and would do everything possible to help me keep my job, but he didn't hold out much hope, since the James Bay project had been the sole reason for hiring me.

Then, showing both concern and apprehension, he suggested that if I really wanted to get out of my financial pit, the James Bay offer was the solution.

While I was listening to him, the old clairvoyant's message echoed in my mind: accept a new offer of work as soon as the chance arose.

- **Was this the opportunity to which the clairvoyant had referred?**
- **How would I know if it was?**

Once again I was confronted with the riddle of decision-making, finding myself in a deepening state of mental confusion.

Then, I asked myself the following questions:
- **If I refused to go to James Bay, would I be able to keep my job with the company in Montreal?**

Immediately, I felt a sensation of fear, confusion, and uncertainty. Something inside of me was trying to make me understand that if I didn't go to James Bay, the company would fire me.

Whenever I asked myself if the company's proposal would make more money for me and was this the opportunity to which the clairvoyant referred, the fear, confusion, and indecision vanished, and in its place was a sense of calm and confidence. Every time I asked myself those questions, I experienced the very same sensations. At first, I paid no attention to these perceptions, but as I continued to experiment with them, I couldn't help but wonder if the feeling of calm and confidence meant the right decision was to go to James Bay—and that it was, in fact, the opportunity the old clairvoyant had in mind for me.

But even if it were the right thing to do, could I go in good conscience, leaving Pina and Pino by themselves in those conditions?

At about one in the afternoon, my boss called and said he had spoken with the general manager, and that although he was sorry to hear about my wife's condition, if I were not able to go to James Bay as scheduled, he would have to let me go. There was just not enough work in Montreal to justify keeping me on. He gave me until that late afternoon to make up my mind.

I told him I would have to think about it. My boss expressed his regret at how things had turned out, but added there was nothing he could do. I thanked him, said I understood, and then went back to work. As I tried to carry on with the tasks at hand, my nerves frazzled into a splitting headache. Once again, the fear of making the wrong decision had left me practically paralyzed.

I didn't not know what to do.

After debating with myself all afternoon, I decided to accept the

James Bay offer. At that very moment, all my malaise—my headache, nervousness, and insecurity—dissipated, and a welcome sense of calm, self-assurance, joy, and an incredible surge of enthusiasm rushed in to take its place.

I could hardly believe this sudden metamorphosis. Now I had no doubt: I was sure this was what the little old clairvoyant had predicted and, without giving the matter any further thought, I went straight to my boss and told him of my decision to go with all the other workers on Saturday night.

Having done this, I was now faced with another tremendous dilemma:

- **Where would I find the strength to tell Pina I had decided to go to James Bay?**
- **How would she interpret my decision?**
- **Was it right to leave her alone with our son, given our precarious living conditions?**
- **Would it be fair to give my priority to work and not to her and our child?**
- **Would she think I lacked understanding and compassion, and that my love for money was far greater than the love I bore her and our child?**
- **Could my sudden decision endanger our relationship or, for that matter, our marriage itself?**

As I asked myself these important questions, confusion and fear assailed me again. Had I made the right decision? At last, I decided to leave for James Bay with or without Pina's approval, in the hope that perhaps—maybe not soon, but one day—she would understand why I had to take such a harsh stand on the matter.

Eventually Pina would realize it was not the love of money that motivated me, but the love I had for her and Pino and my desire to perform my duty as husband and father and offer them a more secure life.

Chapter 24

As head of the family, it was my responsibility to make this crucial decision in our lives. It was important for me to earn as much money as I could to escape the failure that surrounded me and that had brought my life to a standstill. I simply could not afford to give in to the fear of failure one more time.

With these thoughts in mind, and with a ray of hope in my heart that Pina would understand, I kept looking at my watch, thinking about the moment I would be facing Pina.

When I finally got home, I mustered all my strength. Being as sensitive as possible, I explained to Pina that after having seriously reflected on the matter, I had decided to go to James Bay. If I refused, I would lose my job.

She turned around without uttering a word.

I interpreted her silence as a vote of approval. When I went to face her, however, she was crying softly. "I don't have the strength to stay in Montreal by myself," she said, "living in poverty without a refrigerator, a stove or even a table, and having to walk to Maria's house and to the baby-sitter every morning and night."

I told her we had approximately $400.00 in savings. With that we could go to a furniture and electrical store and see if they would sell us what we needed and take a half-payment up front with the balance in thirty days. Pina was doubtful we could find someone willing to work with us. I promptly replied that this was common practice for many stores in Montreal at that time, and we could certainly find one that would be willing to give us credit.

"It wouldn't be the end of the world if you were fired, you know. You could certainly find another job without a problem."

I explained that I didn't want just another job, reminding her of our plans to go back into business. The job at James Bay, I explained, was important for two reasons: I could earn far more money there than in Montreal, and I would be able to gather experience in the field—something that would keep us from falling into the same trap we had in Winnipeg with the clothing store.

Enraged at my logic, she yelled everything I was afraid she would come up with: that I did not love her, that I had no interest in her or in our child, that I was a heartless man lacking in compassion and scruples, and that my ego and love for money was more important to me than she and our son.

Hearing her rave, I finally lost my patience. I screamed back. "Contrary to what you're thinking," I explained, "it is precisely because of my deep love for you and our child that I am willing to sacrifice myself by staying away from you. It is that important to get out from under our financial rut as soon as possible. Furthermore," I said, "I can no longer bear to live under these wretched conditions—I am afraid I might lose my mind."

Without even looking at me, she said, "You are free to do as you wish. This discussion is a waste of our time and breath." Her reaction, completely lacking in objectivity or comprehension of my position, hurt me immensely, even though I understood that her words were spoken in a moment of rage. I continued to hope that one day she would see the facts clearly and understand the true aim of my heart and my thinking, and that she could find forgiveness for me and my actions.

At nine o'clock the next morning, while looking at the paper, I saw an ad from a store that had all we needed. We went to talk to the manager immediately. I explained what we wanted to buy and that we would be able to give him $400 as a down payment with the remainder to be paid in thirty days. He said that was no problem and wrote up the contract. "Delivery is on Monday, if that's okay with you. My delivery man isn't working this weekend." We agreed, signed the contract, gave him the deposit, and left.

Pina and I hardly spoke a word to each other all day. Then, around nine in the evening, a small company van came to pick me up. We barely said goodbye. By midnight, the journey of a thousand miles began. Twenty-eight hours through one continuous forest, we finally arrived in James Bay.

Chapter 24

We were taken to a camp called L.G. 2, where about 4,000 laborers were working. The camp consisted of well-furnished, comfortable mobile homes. There was also a movie theatre, a billiards room, a tavern, and an immense, brand-new cafeteria, which was immaculately clean. The food was excellent and extremely abundant, and there was an incredible variety of dishes to choose from, including soups, roasts, and all sorts of fruit and delicious pastries—enough to satisfy even the most demanding of palates. It would be no exaggeration to say that it compared very favorably with the best restaurants in Montreal. The only problem with the camp was that the telephone service was not good, making it difficult for us to get in touch with our families back home.

A week after my arrival, I was finally able to reach home. Pina greeted the sound of my voice in a most unexpected manner—screaming, yelling, and crying all at once, obviously quite enraged. She managed to express her belief that I should never have left her alone in such a deplorable plight, and was so agitated that I could barely make sense out of what she was saying.

Finally, she explained that on Monday morning the manager of the appliance store had called, informing her that when he took the contract to the store's owner for approval, he refused to okay it on the basis that he didn't know us. Thus, the only thing delivered to the apartment was the refrigerator. After calming her down, I told her how sorry I was, and assured her I would either get an advance on my salary or borrow from one of my co-workers. "Give me a couple of days, and I will have the money. Then you can buy whatever you need. Okay?" Slowly, Pina calmed down and apologized for her rudeness. "It's not your fault," she said. "And there's no need to borrow money because your cousin Theresa's mother-in-law lent me a small electric stove and a little children's table, which suits me fine for now." She went on to say I shouldn't worry, as she knew I was sacrificing myself for Pino and her, and she loved me very much. Then she wanted to know about the food and the working conditions, and if I missed her and Pino as much as they missed me—and if I was thinking about them. I told her I missed them immensely and that what kept me going was the thought of them and the awareness that our sacrifice would eventually lead us to a better life.

This conciliatory conversation brought joy and comfort to my heart, as well as greater hope for the future.

Meanwhile, work progressed well. In fact, we worked an average of twelve hours a day, seven days a week—adding up to a very decent weekly paycheck. At that rate, we would soon be on our way to financial recovery. With the exception of my work mates, the only other creatures I saw around camp were bears. This almost total isolation from the outside world gave me a chance to think about Pina and Pino.

The majority of my fellow workers were Italian, and soon I became friendly with them, especially with my roommate, a fifty-five year-old laborer by the name of Antonio.

He was a calm sort of fellow and spoke very little. Following supper, we sometimes talked a bit, after which he would fall asleep and I would read until late at night. This practice of reading at night somehow attenuated my loneliness for Pina and our child.

One evening, my conversation with Antonio turned to the subject of clairvoyance and an experience he'd had when he left Italy for Canada.

He'd decided to take along some homemade salami and cheese produced in his hometown. Bringing these goods into Canada was illegal, and he worried they might be confiscated. He explained his dilemma to a friend who knew of a man who wrote special letters allowing immigrants to pass through customs without incident.

Antonio went to see the man, who charged him two thousand lire, the equivalent of four dollars at the time, to write such a letter for him. The man wrote it, sealed it, and handed it over to Antonio, instructing him to hide it inside the first suitcase he presented to the customs official. The man told him that as soon as he got off the plane and claimed his luggage, he would be told to proceed straight to customs. In front of him would be a woman dressed in black, whose luggage would be inspected very carefully. When Antonio's turn came, he would be asked to open the first suitcase for what would turn out to be a cursory inspection, after which he would be told to close it and go on his way. The fellow behind him, however, would have all his suitcases searched, and his salami and cheese would be confiscated.

Before Antonio left, the clairvoyant gave him one last piece of advice. "After leaving the airport," he said, "put the letter inside your wallet, because it will always help you find work."

Antonio said that everything he was told came true, just as the clairvoyant had predicted.

The burning questions now was, how did the clairvoyant know this was going to happen in the precise way it did, one week in advance of the event? It's very easy to say that such predictions are simply contrived nonsense from which accurate results are mere coincidence.

But the question was, is that true, or are we making those assumptions in order to explain the unexplainable?

After hearing Antonio's account, I couldn't help relating the experience I'd had with my mother, as well as the more recent one with the ninety-eight year-old clairvoyant in Montreal. We both agreed that even if such phenomena seemed incredible and beyond the bounds of possibility, there were nevertheless people who appeared to have supernatural powers and could put them to use.

After our conversation, Antonio fell immediately to sleep, but I could not. Instead, I thought about my clairvoyant in Montreal and how she knew about my job change and what might have been the key ingredients to finding the path for me to follow.

I analyzed the emotional process I had experienced when I made that fateful decision.

- **Was the perception of peacefulness, the signal that I was doing the right thing?**

- **Was the perception of nervousness and fear a sign that I was on the wrong path?**

To be perfectly honest, my decision to go to James Bay came out of my fear of not being able to find another job right way. At that time, I was hoping to make the right decision. Now, I knew I had.

In order to understand what had happened to me during the decision-making process, I asked myself:
- **Could my feelings have been coincidental, or could they have represented the answers to my questions?**
- **Could it be that peace represented the right thing to do and fear represented the wrong?**

What was the truth?

Inspired by my seemingly innocuous conversation with Antonio that night, I vowed that regardless of how long it took, I would someday unravel the mystery and the answers to those questions.

We remained in James Bay until October 9, when a major snowstorm disrupted our work. During the hundred days I worked at James Bay, I was able to put aside over $13,000.00—a considerable sum for a laborer at that time. On October 10, we all returned to Montreal, where I caught Pina and Pinuccio (Pino's nickname) by surprise, as I had not told them I would be arriving that day.

I had not shaved while I was gone, so I returned to my family looking like a caveman. Needless to say, this new look did not exactly meet with their approval, but it certainly didn't dampen my emotions or theirs. Taking them both into my arms again was one of the happiest moments of my life.

CHAPTER 25

Encounter with a Healer

While I was away, Pina and I had completely made up, realizing once more, that despite all the problems and lack of understanding arising between us at times, our love for each other and for our son, and the desire to keep our family together, were far more important than any temporary misunderstandings. It was time to have another child and give Pino a little brother or sister.

One Monday afternoon, about a week later, I came home from work and assessed our impoverished living conditions. We needed to move into a more decent and comfortable place. I discussed my thoughts with Pina.

"I would love for us to live in a first- or second-floor apartment with a balcony," Pina said. "Then Pino could play in the sunlight and look at the world outside, rather than being forced to stay inside all the time like a mole." Then, heaving a long sigh, she commented that this wish of ours was perhaps impossible, since we could not easily break our contractual obligations with the owner of the apartment we were presently renting.

"If I explain our situation to him and our willingness to pay more rent for one of his other apartments, there's no reason for him to turn us down," I said.

Pina looked less certain than I felt.

"I'll talk to the owner next weekend," I said, smiling. "And don't expect me to return with a 'no.'"

Immediately after this conversation, I visualized moving into a beautiful two-bedroom apartment with a large kitchen and spacious living room, nicely furnished, and located on the second floor of a new triplex. For the next two days, day and night, I continually rehearsed how I would approach the owner that coming weekend, and what I would say to him.

On Thursday afternoon, I got home from work a bit earlier than usual, and found a note from the apartment owner in our mailbox. He said he wanted to talk to me about something important, and asked me to come to his office as soon as I could.

Since his office was not too far from our apartment and Pina had not yet returned from work, I decided to go see him right way.

He greeted me with a big smile, and after asking how I was doing, he said he had an important proposal to discuss. I asked what it was all about, and he explained he had an interested buyer for the building we lived in, but the individual would not consider the purchase unless the apartment in which I was living were vacant, as the buyer needed the flat for his parents. If I were willing to move, he would rent me another apartment consisting of two bedrooms, a large dining room, a beautiful adjacent kitchen, and front and back balconies at the second floor in a brand new triplex located not far from where I was living now.

After a pause, he said the cost would be the same as my little apartment; not only that, but he would extend the lease for another year at the same rent and terms. Anxiously, and without even giving me a chance to respond, he asked what I thought about the deal. I couldn't believe what I was hearing. I was extremely happy, but listened quietly without betraying emotion. Unable to fathom what was going through my mind, and in a heightened state of anxiety, he asked me to please help him out so he would be able to sell the building.

Finally, I smiled and told him I would be happy to help him out, and I would accept his proposal and vacate the apartment that very weekend.

The tension faded from his face as he shook my hand. Within ten minutes, we had signed the new contract. I practically ran all the way home.

Chapter 25

Pina had already arrived from work. Seeing me so happy, she asked what had happened.

"Guess," I said.

She did, but to no avail. After a few tries, I said, "You're never going to come up with the right answer." I handed over the envelope, asking her to read the letter inside. As she read, she shook her head, incredulous about our good fortune. We both wondered if there was more than coincidence at work here.

That weekend we moved into the new apartment, and went out and bought new furniture. Now we could invite friends and family to visit.

Around that time, a friend from work told me his wife was ill and the doctors were unable to determine the cause. Someone recommended she see a healer in Ottawa, but they had no car. He asked if I would drive them on my day off. Of course, I agreed to do it.

The healer, a man in his fifties, received my friend's wife warmly and treated her in private. Afterwards, she said she was feeling better.

We were ready to leave when my curiosity got the best of me, and I asked the healer how he'd discovered his ability to heal the sick.

"It's a divine gift," he replied, "I inherited it from my father before he died."

"Do you know what a clairvoyant is?" I asked.

"Yes. In fact, I am one."

"Is there anything you can tell me about myself?"

He looked into my eyes for an instant, then said, "You came in this world to be an employer and not an employee." After a moment, he added, "Do not worry, Paolo. Keep going on the path you are on, and one day, your dreams will become reality."

On the return trip to Montreal, the familiar questions flooded my mind:

- **Who was responsible for a healer's abilities?**
- **Is it truly a special gift from God?**
- **Why would God—provided there was a God—bestow such**

special favors on a select few, and leave everyone else in the dark?
- Who was this God who operated in such a peculiar manner?
- Were these riddles an example of His fairness?

With the passage of time, my curiosity grew into enormous craving for the truth. I believed there was a rational explanation for everything, but the more I looked for it, the deeper I plunged into the darkness of confusion. One day I turned my eyes towards the heavens and said,

"God, if You really exist and are all-knowing, I beseech You to take pity on me in my confusion and to guide me toward the key to Your eternal mysteries."

After reciting this short prayer for approximately twenty minutes, a great sense of peace enveloped me. My compulsive desire to find the answers ceased to bother me.

Winter arrived, and with it snow and cold weather, which made working outside impossible. So, we were discharged from our jobs and I applied for unemployment compensation.

Pina became sick with frequent bouts of nausea and vomiting—and we soon received the happy news that she was pregnant. I advised her to stop working at the factory, as the heavy work schedule would benefit neither her nor the baby she was carrying. She agreed, and a few days later informed the factory owner. He said that if she wanted to work at home as she could, he would supply her with a sewing machine and the materials. She said she would think it over and let him know.

That night we talked it over and agreed the extra money would help pay for everyday expenses without forcing us to dip into our savings. The following day, she told the company owner she accepted his offer. A few days later she began to work at home—a welcome development, considering the season and the fact that I had been laid off. With the extra time on my hands, I helped her as much as possible, and whenever necessary, I did the household chores.

Our lives were taking a turn for the better. There was greater harmony in our household, and our future looked rosier. We talked about what to do with our small savings. I planned to save them so I could eventually start a small asphalt-paving company.

Pina thought we should buy a house in which we could raise our children.

Once again I was caught up in the old quandary of a decision.

I noticed that whenever I thought of buying the house I felt calm and secure; whereas when I thought of saving the money for starting a business, I felt insecure, nervous, and confused.

I recalled the experience I'd had before leaving for James Bay and the message from the old clairvoyant in which she assured me I would know the right thing to do.

Now, if the perception of peace and harmony meant I was on the right track, I was losing confidence in her advice, as I was convinced that if I were to form a company and become a contractor, I would earn far more money than I could as a laborer. Then, not only would I achieve the goal of having my own business, but of buying a house, as well. If, on the other hand, I bought a house with our savings, I would get the family settled, but I would not have money to start my own business and I'd remain a laborer with a limited salary.

So, while going into business made sense logically, I wondered why my intuition, which had worked successfully for me before, was now apparently leading me in the opposite direction. I spoke with Pina about my concern. After reflecting on the matter for some time, she told me how she felt—that the best thing to do at that moment was to buy the house, thereby putting an end to our roaming and allowing us to enjoy a more stable, secure, and perhaps happier existence.

I sensed that Pina was right, and for the first time in my life I perfectly understood that family stability was far more important than

Our Six Apartment Complex at 11367 Balzac Road, Montreal.

going into business. I then knew with certainty the best decision was to follow our intuition to buy a house.

We spoke with a few real estate agents, telling them what we wanted and how much we had available for a down payment. A few days later, one of the agents called. He had found a building with three apartments in the Old Montreal neighborhood. The price was excellent and the down payment was reasonable. But even though the house was a bit old for our tastes, we decided it would be a good investment as we could rent out two of the apartments, which would pay for our mortgage and taxes, and we could live in the third apartment rent-free. So, we bought it.

Soon after, another real estate agent called, informing us he had found a small block of flats consisting of six practically new apartments in the city of Montreal North. The building faced a large, beautiful city park, and the price was extremely low. Because the owner was sick and his children showed no interest in the property, his wife had decided to sell it. I told the realtor he was a bit too late since we had bought another property. He promptly replied that such bargains rarely materialized in the real estate market and he wanted us to have a chance to see it. Pina and I decided to take a look.

The agent was right—it was truly a beautiful building—the adjacent grounds were marvelous and the price was fantastic. Chances like that surely didn't come around every day. We desperately wanted to buy it, but by now we didn't have enough money to make the down payment.

So I called Gioacchino and asked him to inquire at the bank, where we had been long-standing clients, to see if the manager would give us a loan. The next day Gioacchino called me back, informing me the bank manager agreed to the loan. The strangest thing about the deal was that because the owner owned the building free and clear, he was willing to carry the note on the condition we would make payments on an annual basis rather than monthly. I bought the complex on that basis. Meanwhile, the apartments were rented and the leases were due to expire at the end of April. Since the lease on our own apartment wouldn't expire until approximately the same time, we had to wait until then before we could move into one of our newly-purchased apartments.

I could hardly believe the good luck that had befallen me. In a few months' time our fate seemed finally headed in the right direction. Pina continued sewing leather jackets, and I helped her with the housework. Between the money she was earning and my unemployment compensation, we led a relatively comfortable life.

It was during this period of time that my desire to understand the mystery of life and to find the answers to all those questions that had trouble me for most of my life became very strong.

One day I went to Pina's factory to drop off her finished work and pick up a new collection. For no apparent reason, I was very nervous. On the way home, being near St. Hubert Street, which at the time was the best-known shopping area in the city, I randomly decided to park the car and go for a stroll. I walked aimlessly, looking at shop windows and admiring the various objects on display. I passed a bookstore, scanned a few book covers, then resumed my pace. After walking another three hundred feet, I felt an irresistible force turning me around and directing me back to the bookstore.

As I entered, my sense of nervousness ceased. An elderly shopkeeper greeted me with a friendly smile and asked if there was anything she could do for me and if I were looking for any book in particular. Rather surprised at myself for being there in the first place, and therefore slightly embarrassed, I said I simply wanted to look around.

She replied I was perfectly welcome to do so, and then she stepped away. I browsed the shelves aimlessly, pretending to be searching for a special book. My eyes settled on two volumes: *How to Become a Clairvoyant* and *The Wonders of the Spirit World*.

As I read the above words, my heart beat faster and faster. I skimmed through each volume, stopping to read the various chapter headings. Then I asked the storekeeper the price of the books.

"Forty-five each," was her reply.

"That's too much," I said.

She laughed and agreed with me.

Pina averaged about ninety dollars a week for the work she was doing at home. My internal debate began—should I or shouldn't I buy those two books? Was it wise to spend that much money on them? Finally, curiosity took the upper hand and I decided to purchase them, hoping Pina wouldn't be furious with me.

Once home, I told Pina I had bought the books, and then related the entire episode. She said it seemed strange, but never bothered to ask how much I spent, and I didn't volunteer. Relieved, I changed the subject, and that was that.

I spent the following days reading the books. When I got through, I was disappointed, as there was nothing in them I didn't already know and, despite the titles, there were no techniques revealed on how to become a clairvoyant.

Two weeks later on my way back from Pina's factory, I felt an urge to return to the bookstore. The same shopkeeper greeted me and asked about the books. I told her I was disappointed, that despite their titles they offered no techniques for becoming clairvoyant. That I had paid so much for them made it even more upsetting.

She thought for a moment, and then excused herself. When she came back, she carried a small book in her hands "*The Power of Your Subconscious Mind*" by Joseph Murphy. "You'll find this one much more interesting than the others, and it's only three dollars and ninety-five cents."

When I heard the price, I laughed. "I think I can manage this one without risking the wrath of my wife." I paid for the book, and promised I would read it and give her my reaction.

When Pina saw me with the new book, she cautioned me not to get involved in the occult. I assured her I was not. I also eased her mind by telling her the price of the book. She joked and said that if I didn't want any trouble with her, I'd better help her prepare supper.

That same evening I began reading the new book, which turned out to be interesting enough that I would read it through three times over the next few days.

In my own words and the way I remember the book, the author's theory was this:

Man is made up of two distinct components: one visible and one invisible. The visible part is represented by the body—the majority of whose functions we have come to understand. The invisible part consists of two separate elements: the conscious mind, whose task it is to make us think and therefore create thoughts; and the subconscious mind, the Creative Power in man whose function is to create, to externalize, and to manifest in our lives whatever our minds have created and conceived in the form of thoughts.

Consequently, the conditions we find ourselves in, good or bad are brought exclusively by the thoughts we create and cultivate in our minds.

The author was affirming that when we are dissatisfied with our plight, we can simply change it by creating with our mind those thoughts that best reflect the conditions we desire, and changes will follow.

For example, if a man is poor and wants to be rich, he must first determine the amount of wealth he wants to acquire. Then, by constantly repeating his objective—and without ever doubting, tiring, being overtaken by fear, or altering his aim—in time, that special invisible essence embedded in his being will provide the proper conditions to make his wish come true.

Along the same line of thought, if a person is sick and wants to be healthy—no matter how grave the condition or how poor the doctor's prognosis, as long as he/she has a firm and fervent belief that he/she would be cured, the individual's invisible essence will provide the proper conditions for restoration of health.

Thus, if instead of thinking positively a person dwells on the negative aspects of life—poor health, poverty, failure, unhappiness—

that same invisible essence will provide the conditions necessary to transform those thoughts into reality, and deliver that person into the depths of misery.

In conclusion, what I had just learned was that:

Our minds and thoughts are the only instruments responsible for our fortunes and misfortunes, successes and failures, happiness and misery, good health and sickness—and that in the final analysis we are the prime and only movers of all the circumstances and conditions we experience in our life, good or bad as they may be. And that consciously or unconsciously, through the use of our free will, we direct and shape the course of our lives and the conditions under which we live.

Hence, according to the author:

We must constantly monitor and control the type of thoughts we create.

I had trouble believing the author's theory, and I occasionally laughed out loud as I read his outrageous precepts. At the time, it was nearly impossible for me to fathom how our thoughts, abstract as they are, could control every aspect of our lives.

Could life, as complicated and mysterious as it appears, really be that simple?

As the days passed, however, I considered the possibilities. When I mulled over the notion that our thoughts were in charge of our lives, I felt infused by a sense of tranquility. But when I doubted the author's conclusions, I felt nervous and uncertain.

This ambivalence brought to mind the quandary I faced before going to James Bay, when I couldn't decide whether or not to go, and the dilemma of buying the house as opposed to investing the money in a business. If the sense of peace and tranquility I felt resulted from my inner essence trying to convey to me the right course of action, then the conclusion could only be that what I had learned in the book was true.

A serious psychological struggle ensued within me. On the one hand, my intuition was directing me to believe, and therefore put into practice, what I had learned. On the other, my unenlightened reasoning rebelled, causing me to think that whatever I had learned in the book was nothing but a heap of garbage. Unable to make up my mind, I sought clarification by analyzing my past experiences.

Every time I had untiringly applied myself towards reaching a goal—without deviating from my path or entertaining doubts—everything I had hoped for and eagerly desired came to fruition.

One example was my return to school in Sicily and another was bringing my family together in North America.

At the same time, however, not everything I had ardently desired had come to pass. During my father's long illness, my family prayed constantly for his healing. What was the result? After so much suffering, he died. Then there was the matter of my financial success, which I so deeply desired. Again, what was the outcome? Nine years after leaving Sicily and working hard toward my goal, all I had to show for it was sacrifice and disillusionment.

The author affirmed that disease was a direct result of man's indulgence in negative thinking. If that were the case, however, how does one explain the physical and psychological imperfections affecting newborn infants?

Are babies, at birth, already the agents of their own misfortunes and ailments?

Furthermore, an enormous number of terminally ill people of faith pray to regain their health. How many of those actually succeed in getting well?

For the most part, their prayers and hopes fade into thin air, leaving their death sentence intact.

In light of these considerations, I doubted the author's premises and felt confused.

The plight I found myself in gave me the fatalistic notion that—

somehow or other—destiny predetermines our lives and compels us to undergo certain existential experiences. Hence our trials and vicissitudes are not related to our thoughts, but are directed instead by uncontrollable, mysterious forces tossing us around like ships in a raging storm, which, in the majority of instances, our minds are unable to control.

Having reached this harsh conclusion, I continued to lead my daily routine without further scrutiny of my thought processes, since I was convinced that any further research would be an exercise in futility.

Nino's Baptism in 1976 in Montreal.
From left: Joe & Angie Salvo (God Parents) Nino, Pina, and myself. In the front from the left is Pasqualino Salvo (Joe's Nephew) and our son Pino.

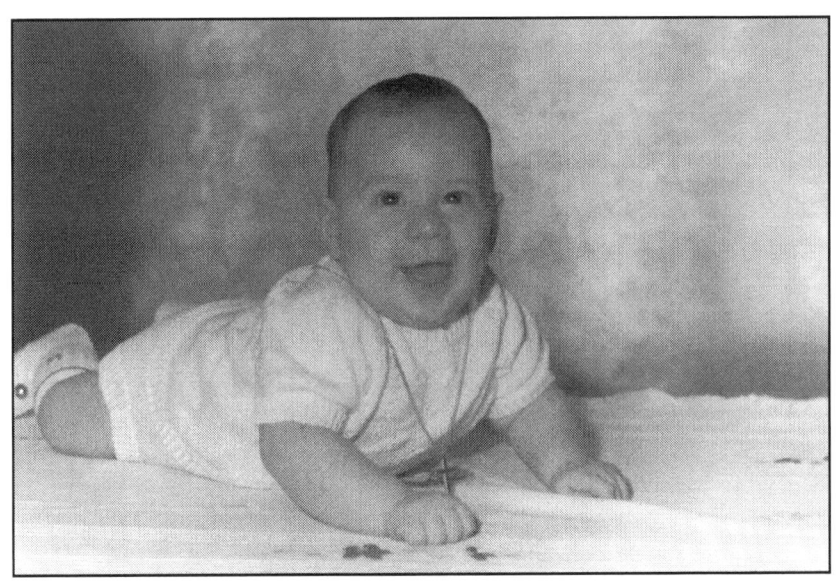

Our second child, Antonino Nino Ficara – two months old, Montreal, 1976.

Pina, our Son Nino, myself, and our son Pino on the day of Nino's baptism. Montreal 1976.

CHAPTER 26
Second Child, First Healing

The end of January 1976 was approaching, and our family was doing fine. When she felt well enough, Pina sewed leather jackets for the factory, and I helped her as much as I could. Meanwhile, her belly grew larger.

One day as I stopped at an Italian café shop and saw my friend Rocco. After the usual greetings, he asked where I would be working in the spring. I replied I didn't know, but surely I would want to work for a small asphalt-paving company. He disagreed, saying it was better to work for a large company for two reasons: first, they offered security and stability; and second, smaller companies required owners to be on-site, and that translated into having to work longer and harder.

"Oh, I'm already aware of that," I said and laughed.

Rocco asked why I wanted to work for a small company, then.

I confided that if everything went according to plan, by the spring of 1977 I would be starting my own asphalt-paving company. "Why wait until 1977? Why not start this spring?" he asked.

I explained to Rocco I was in no condition to put my plan into action right now due to three primary deficiencies—funds, experience, and psychological maturity. Recollecting my dismal experience in Winnipeg, I told him I had to be very careful, because if things didn't work out, the negative effects could destroy me psychologically. For that reason, I had to pay attention to what I was doing and avoid another financial fiasco. I explained that working for a small company, would give the possibility to learn first-hand the problems related to the business, to get better acquainted with the environment, to get to know the general contractors and the learn the areas of the city undergoing major development. These were essential features to know well if I wanted to succeed in that business. Furthermore, since I had already exhausted my savings with the purchase of two houses, I needed a year to save the money I would need for the equipment.

After listening to me carefully, Rocco said my way of thinking made sense and showed maturity of judgment. Had I been willing to begin this spring, he said he would have been happy to partner with me in my projected venture.

"I'm honored by your trust in me," I said, "but I already have a partner in my brother Gioacchino. We've worked together most of our lives, and he's in the U.S. right now waiting for me."

Rocco knew Gioacchino—he had worked with him in a textile manufacturing plant in 1968, when Gioacchino had just arrived from Germany. He said he respected my brother very much and would be pleased to have him as a partner as well.

Rocco suggested we embark on our adventure and let Gioacchino join us whenever he could.

"In that case," I replied, "there is no problem, and we'll get our company going as soon as possible."

Then Rocco told me that he knew the owners of several small companies. If I wanted him to, he could find work for both of us.

The whole plan was fantastic, I thought. After a handshake, we parted.

Back home, I told Pina about the agreement I had reached with Rocco. She was overjoyed, remarking how good it was for me to share my responsibilities with someone.

A few weeks later Rocco dropped over. He said he had found a company willing to give us work by the end of March, when the snows started melting. This news lifted my morale quite a bit, and I began to look to the future with more optimism, in the hope that this time things would work out for the best.

At the end of March, we started working. After approximately a month on the job, we learned another company was looking for laborers and offering better wages—and its working conditions approximated the ones we planned to implement in our own business. We gave our employer notice, and began working for the new company.

In the meantime, we bought a small, old truck in reasonable condition for three hundred dollars and began doing small concrete jobs on weekends, allowing us to save additional money.

At the beginning of May, Pina, Pino and I moved into one of the apartments we had purchased in Montreal North. During the previous year-and-a-half, we had roamed and suffered and changed residences twelve times. It was good to finally settle down in our own little home, which offered the security, tranquility and hope we so badly needed.

Meanwhile, Pina's belly was growing and we were anxiously waiting for the month of July when our baby was to be born. The doctor assured us that everything was proceeding normally, but warned that as soon as Pina's contractions began, I should take her to the hospital immediately, since he estimated her labor to be relatively quick. Heeding the doctor's advice, I constantly told Pina where I could be found and how I could be reached.

Finally, on July 10 at nine in the morning, I got a message at work to call home. Pina had suffered a hemorrhage and her contractions had begun. I told her to remain calm and to telephone my cousin Pasquale, Maria's husband, who had a small store near our house. He could take her to the hospital and I would meet her there.

At the hospital, the hours ticked by. The labor pains had come and gone, but our baby had not arrived. By ten o'clock in the evening, Pina said she no longer had any pains. I told the nurse, who checked the monitor and confirmed the contractions had stopped. She called the doctor, who ordered x-rays. A fibroma in Pina's uterus was obstructing the passage of the baby through the birth canal. He would have to perform an emergency C-section to save the lives of both baby and mother.

I signed the necessary authorization and then began my vigil in the waiting room. Considering the dire possibilities, I was extremely nervous and instinctively prayed to God. Finally, at a quarter to midnight, the nurse arrived carrying a white blanket wrapped around a beautiful baby. Pina had given birth to a boy and everything had gone very well. The doctor would be coming soon to see me and answer any questions I might have. After hearing the good news, I gave a sigh of relief, and with my heart overflowing with joy, I thanked God.

When the doctor arrived, he offered his congratulations and explained that there had been two fibroid tumors inside the uterus, one large and one small. He removed the large one, but thought it was best to leave the smaller one alone for now. I asked him what had caused the complication. With a puzzled look he replied he didn't know, and then left. At the nurse's station I inquired about Pina's room number, and then spent the next hour there waiting for her to show up.

After Pina recovered from the anesthesia, we discussed baby names. Out of respect for our tradition, we chose Antonino (Nino), after Pina's father.

It was very late when I arrived home. My mother was there with Pino. I filled her in on all the details, including the tumor and the emergency surgery. Then I awakened two-year-old Pino and told him he had a little brother with whom he could play.

"When can I meet him?" he wanted to know.

"Tomorrow," I promised, "at the hospital."

After a while, I went to bed, but I just couldn't sleep. My mind was filled with the events of the day.

- **How was it possible that Pina's doctor, one of the best gynecologists in Montreal, had not discovered the uterine tumor at some point during Pina's pregnancy?**
- **What could have been its cause?**

I contemplated the theory I had read during the winter about the power of our thoughts:

Anything we conceive with emotion and intensity in the form of thoughts is transmitted to the invisible Creative Power within us, and in due time will manifest in our lives in the form of experience.

I thought of the excuse I had fabricated a year earlier when I'd told my boss Pina suffered from a fibroid tumor. Did that lie have any connection with Pina's fibroid tumor, or was it merely a coincidence?

After a few days, Pina and Nino were dismissed from the hospital and we began our lives as an expanded family, but my thoughts continued to revisit that tormenting question:

Was it possible there was a link between my thinking and Pina's tumor?

Whenever I inquired if my thoughts had been responsible for Pina's problems, I felt a sense of great calm. When I thought instead it was impossible to have a connection between my mind and the events—that it had simply been the result of coincidence—I felt nervous and apprehensive.

What I had learned through my own experience the previous year was that the perception of peace and tranquility translated into the right thing to do or to accept, whereas nervousness signaled I had a false perception. Interpreting what I felt this time in the same light as before, I was faced with the conclusion that my thoughts were the cause and the origin of Pina's fibroid tumor.

I was shocked.

Once again I could not help wondering how my thoughts, abstract conceptions as they were, could have the power to generate such a serious, tangible illness in the body of another human being.

How could this be?

Notwithstanding this convincing analysis and the lessons of my own experience, I still refused to accept my own conclusions. But the more I thought about the puzzle the more I became scared and frustrated by my inability to understand the message my intuition sent me.

When finally I took responsibility for Pina's tumor, the feelings of guilt plunged me into a psychological crisis.

One night while resting on the sofa and examining what I had learned, I asked myself:

- **If we are solely responsible for our lives, destinies, and experiences, what is the function of that entity we commonly address as God?**
- **How does one explain the fact that for thousands of years civilized man has believed in a God that influences our lives and destiny?**
- **Could all these people be wrong?**
- **Who is God in His true essence?**

Unfortunately, I could not find adequate answers to these queries and I continued to struggle with my doubts until I finally wearied of the guilt over Pina's tumor. As I considered the possibility that my perception was true, I turned to God for help:

"God, even if I don't know who You are or if You really exist, I beg You to deliver me from the pain and fear that constantly haunts me."

After repeating that prayer a few times, all the painful anxiety I had felt suddenly vanished, and I was imbued with a great sense of relief and indescribable peace.

That, to me, was a sign it was time to forget the past and start practicing what I had learned. I began, continuously and indefatigably, to analyze the nature of all my thoughts in order to cultivate those that corresponded with my genuine desires, and to neutralize or discard those that could only cause me pain.

Furthermore, if the principles I had learned were truly valid, then a person who was sick could be healed by simply praying for recovery, and a person who was poor could achieve financial success by praying to be rich and eliminating the doubts of his own abilities to make that happen.

I imagined the thrill of seeing sick people cured, or their suffering alleviated. What greater sense of satisfaction could one have in this life?

In putting everything I had learned into practice, I prayed incessantly, believing in my heart that all my work and my efforts would be crowned with great success.

To that end, I wrote the following prayer:

"My God, if You really exist and are truly all-knowing, then You are already aware of my thoughts, dreams, and aspirations. And, if You can really accomplish everything, I beg You to guide, inspire, and help me make those decisions that in time will make all my dreams come true."

Instinctively, even though I wasn't sure about God's existence, nor was I sure if God had anything to do with it, I always started my prayer directed to God.

I repeated this little prayer whenever I could—while I was driving, while I was working, while I was watching TV, and at night before falling asleep.

One day I drove past the bookstore and stopped in to say "hi" to the shopkeeper. As we were speaking, I noticed a small booklet titled "Spiritual Healing." I bought it and went straight home to read it.

The author explained that every human being is capable of releasing energy through his hands. This flow of energy is imbued with power capable of healing the sick. The method works as follows: hold your hands close to the diseased part of the body without touching it, and then pray to God for healing. The healing energy flows from the hands to the diseased body. If the sick individual is perfectly attuned to the healer, he will immediately be cured of his illness.

The booklet also mentioned the subject of hemorrhage. If somebody is bleeding and the remedy at hand doesn't stop the blood flow, the solution would be to stare with intensity at that part of the body from which the blood is flowing and either mentally or verbally order the blood to stop. In that moment, the blood will immediately comply with the demand and block its own flow.

I could hardly stop shaking my head, wondering how anyone could believe that a serious physical event like a hemorrhage could be simply and easily stopped by such a banal procedure. Was I reading a fairy tale, or was this writer serious?

For some time, Pina had been complaining about knee pain but had procrastinated about going to a doctor. One evening after I got back from work, she said, "I hope you can take me to the doctor tomorrow. The pain in my knee has gotten worse and I can barely stand it anymore."

Without thinking, I told her there was nothing to worry about. "I will pray for you tonight, and by tomorrow your pain will be gone."

She burst into laughter, thinking I was kidding. Without being the least bit perturbed, I warned that her attitude might have a negative effect on my intervention.

Pina wasn't buying my "mumbo jumbo," and insisted that I take her to the doctor on the following day so she could get the necessary prescriptions. I promised I would. "But in the meanwhile," I said, "why don't we try a little prayer? What can we lose other than a bit of time?"

She conceded I might be right, but she doubted it strongly, non-believer that she was in what she called "voodoo garbage." "Furthermore," she said, "you will not perform any experiments on me."

That could have been the end of the story, but since I was stubborn, I repeated, "We have nothing to lose."

"We'll talk about it at bedtime," she said, and immediately changed the subject.

As we got ready for bed that evening, I reminded her it was time to start praying.

She smiled. "How many times do I have to tell you I'm not interested in your performing any voodoo experiments on me?"

Putting up with her stubbornness now, and not willing to abandon my plan, I patiently told her one more time that we had nothing to lose and that it was worth a try.

After a slight hesitation, she looked at me with a smile. "It's possible you're right." Her smile broadened. "Okay, you win."

After we climbed into bed, I moved close to her, putting my right hand approximately two inches away from her affected knee. Then, closing my eyes, I prayed as follows:

"My God, I am sure You already know the problem with Pina's knee. I therefore beseech You to heal it, restoring the perfection that You originally envisioned there."

As I said this prayer, I was not only willfully admitting God's existence, but, by stating that He already knew what was wrong with Pina's knee and asking Him to cure it, I also acknowledged His Omniscience and Omnipotence. Hence, after so much doubt and confusion in my quest for God, I was finally able to manifest my complete trust in Him without the slightest trace of negativity or doubt.

As I lay beside Pina, I noticed her watching me with amusement. After about twenty minutes, perhaps inspired by the expression on my face, she laughingly suggested that maybe I wasn't the kind of saint who performed miracles. I burst out laughing, too, and so ended our experiment. We talked about how peaceful it was with Nino asleep.

Then, suddenly, Nino started to cry. Pina went to the adjoining bedroom where the children slept, changed the baby's diaper, and fed him. She returned to our bedroom with a somewhat shocked expression on her face, gave me a serious look, and announced, "The pain in my knee is less than before."

I thought she was trying to mock me, but she assured me she was telling the truth. She walked back and forth a few times, putting pressure on her knee. "The pain is still there, but it's very mild," she said. We were both surprised by this turn of events and remained silent for a while. Then I asked her if she had felt anything strange or unusual when we were saying the prayer. Reflecting a while, she was able to recall a slight tingling sensation, combined with some form of heat on that part of her knee that hurt the most.

While I was praying, I had felt that same sensation in the palm of my hand. Naturally, we wondered if her change for the better had anything to do with our prayer or if, again, it was a matter of coincidence. It was a very difficult question to answer. We went to sleep, accepting what had happened without attempting to understand its mechanisms.

This apparently insignificant experience that many people would have ignored made me think deeply. If the healing of Pina's knee was truly the consequence of my prayer, I would be able to repeat the healing any time I chose.

If, on the other hand, Pina's healing was a mere coincidence, I would not be able to do it again.

How would I know the truth? The answer was easy: I had to try again.

The idea of such a challenge made me ecstatic. Thus, with hope in my heart, I waited for a new healing opportunity to come my way.

CHAPTER 27
Our Own Company

Meanwhile, time passed swiftly. It was already the first week in August 1976, and everything was proceeding quite well. Rocco and I still worked for the same company, and on weekends we did small, private jobs. The old truck we had acquired for three hundred dollars continued to serve us faithfully.

I took up the habit of frequently repeating short prayers that revolved around daily problems and focused on what I wanted most to accomplish—success in business. I filled my mind with thoughts of owning my own company with many employees, an image that was vivid enough to seem real. Even though I could distinguish my prayers from reality, the great joy they gave me bolstered my hopes for the future.

One morning at work, I was assigned to help another crew for the day. Later in the day, the company owner came by on the job. He was furious to see the foreman had made some mistakes. Instead of taking it out on the foreman, he unfairly directed his rage at me. I told him he was barking up the wrong tree, and he fired back that my outburst would probably cost me my job. Naturally, it bothered me that my livelihood might be affected, but I was not sorry about my reaction. The man had no right to offend me without justification.

After work, I phoned Rocco and told him what had happened. I also informed him I didn't intend to return to work on the following day—I would be looking for another job instead.

He said not to worry, that he would clarify my position with Luigi, the employer's son, and if that didn't work, he would quit as well, and we would look for another job together. I couldn't help feeling moved by Rocco's loyalty and the support of good friends when you need them the most. This incident reminded me of my dear friends Enzo Tortorici and Giuseppe Zabbara in Ribera, who were always ready to come to my aid whenever I needed them.

After hearing Rocco's response on the phone, Luigi told him to calm down and asked that we both go to his office for a meeting.

About an hour later we all got together with Luigi, his father, and the engineer for the company. By then, Luigi's father had realized he'd accused the wrong person, assured me he had no intention of firing me, and hoped I would agree to stay on. Luigi had learned about my diploma that afternoon, so he asked if it were true I had a land surveyor's diploma, and I assured him it was. He wondered why I had not mentioned that fact to him earlier. I simply shrugged.

The engineer, who was following the discussion, asked if I was capable of reading blueprints and if I could establish survey land elevations on the field. I told him I had studied them in school but had no practical or field experience. After a moment of thinking, he asked me if I would be interested in helping him out if he was willing to teach me. In that case, I said I would. He said he would appreciate my coming to his office the following morning, and if it worked out, I would be given a dollar-an-hour raise, and would not have to return to the asphalt-laying crew.

As I drove home, all the strange events of the day came to my mind. I found it hard to comprehend the irony of what had happened. The argument with the company owner that almost got me fired, had instead contributed toward a possible promotion and the acquiring of valuable experience, which I would not have gotten as long as I remained a laborer. By the time I got home, I was filled with hope, and couldn't wait to tell Pina about my bizarre story and its upbeat ending.

That night, I couldn't fall asleep, worried about the challenges the next day would bring. I feared I would not be able to perform what was required of me, and that the whole opportunity would turn into a huge fiasco.

I remembered the process by which we experience, manifest, and accomplish exactly what we think. I realized that if I wanted to succeed in my new adventure I had to replace all negative thoughts engulfing my mind. So I put all my effort into convincing myself that I had the preparation and the capability of doing the work offered me, and that I would execute it with good results.

I repeated this affirmation until, overtaken by exhaustion, I fell asleep.

The following day the engineer accompanied me to my new assignment, explained what he expected of me, and left. When he returned in the afternoon to inspect my work, he said, "I'm very impressed with the precision and diligence with which you've carried out my orders—even better than I'd hoped."

His words came like the sound of victory.

This experience convinced me that all I had learned in the near past about the mechanics of our thoughts were a wonderful reality.

I believed that part of my success was due to the efficacy of the prayer I had recited the night before and the ability to get rid of my negative thoughts. What made me more enthusiastic and filled with hope was the knowledge that I could repeat the process at will any time I chose.

On that occasion, I promised to myself to pray every day with the conviction that my luck had changed, and henceforth I would attract only happiness and success.

Soon after, I noticed a change in my behavior. My chronic fear of making mistakes now gave way to greater trust in my personal attributes and capabilities, making me considerably more self-confident. I no longer experienced those moments of deep depression that at times caused me to feel life was without purpose. I was discovering a deep new love for life and an enormous desire to enjoy it.

My thoughts would often go to Pina, our children, my mother and my brothers, and the sacrifices they all endured on my behalf and the faith they had that I would lead them to a better future. Now, I was more motivated than ever to overcome any obstacles that stood in the way of achieving my predetermined goals.

It was during this period of elation that I was involved in an automobile crash. Luckily, I suffered no harm, but my car was completely smashed. The timing could not have been worse for my finances, and I needed a way to get back and forth from work. Fortunately, we still had the old truck, which Rocco said I could use for as long as I needed.

Meanwhile, the company was involved with a complex job and the foreman had trouble reading the work plans. The engineer suggested I supervise the job, but it would entail my managing over twenty-five workers. I told him I had no experience at that level of management, but he assured me I had the necessary skills and that he would come out every day to see if I needed his help and to be sure everything was running smoothly.

That night, despite my eagerness to accept this new challenge, once more I was overtaken by the fear of making mistakes and of not being capable of overseeing the entire crew. I began to question whether or not I had the ability to undertake such heavy responsibility or if I had the strength, the character, and the capacity to take on such a task.

I knew from experience that most foremen were stern and disrespectful toward the people they managed. I also knew I was not capable of treating people that way. Perhaps that was the main reason for my fear. Then I began to pray, just as I had in the past, until I was exhausted and fell asleep.

Next morning I was still a little nervous, so before going to work, I drew a mental image that everything would be all right. Those first few days were difficult, but I kept praying to God to guide me and make sure that everything would be all right.

From the first day, I treated workers exactly as I would have liked to be treated—with respect and dignity. So, when somebody made a mistake, instead of scolding or lecturing him, I calmly explained what he was doing wrong and encouraged him to do better the next time. I noticed that when the workers were treated fairly, they were happier and more productive. Naturally, the engineer was satisfied with the results.

As I was helping a worker out one afternoon, the owner of the company showed up at the job site. Seeing me doing manual work, he called me aside and told me I was too good with the workers, that I should be much sterner, and that I should keep my distance, because my behavior could be interpreted as fear or weakness of character.

I disagreed with him, explaining that although I did not have all the experience and assuredness of a veteran foreman, I was getting from the workers the kind of efficiency and response that surpassed their previous performances. I went on to explain that if one was too harsh or rude with the workers, they became resentful, which tended to erode their productivity. I assured him I was not being weak—I merely preferred courtesy and good manners to rudeness.

The owner and I operated on two different wavelengths. It disturbed me that he was more concerned with the respectful way I treated the workers than with the productivity that resulted. I spoke with the engineer about the situation, and he told me not to worry because management was aware of what a superior job I was doing. So I continued to treat the workers with respect and I continued to get the same results.

Meanwhile, a new worker was hired who did the same type of work as Rocco. From Day One, the new man tried to make himself look like the better worker by putting Rocco down whenever he could. Rocco was concerned the new guy was after his job, and one night after work he asked me to come to his house so he could talk over his concerns.

"Ever since that new worker was hired," Rocco said, "the foreman has been treating me unfairly, assigning me the most menial jobs, and reprimanding me for no apparent reason."

I reminded him why we were working there, and that we had only a few months before winter. After that we would be on our own, I explained, starting out with our own small company.

"You're right. I'll try not to let it get to me, and just keep my focus on the future."

Meanwhile, at work, I kept my eye on what was going on, and discovered Rocco was right. The new worker had been hired to replace him. But because it wouldn't look good for the owner to fire a paisano—someone from his hometown in Italy— he instructed his foreman to give Rocco a hard time so he would become frustrated enough to quit on his own.

I was outraged by the owner's deviousness, but forced myself not to show it. Soon, the job would be behind us, and we would both be moving on by our own choice.

One day not long after my discovery, Rocco came over to my job site to tell me he could no longer take the verbal abuse and he had decided to quit before he lost his temper and took a punch at the foreman. I told him he was acting wisely and I would see him later that night at his house.

But that evening after work, I decided to visit the engineer instead, who, as turned out, was not in. Though I had promised Rocco I would visit him, I was too filled with disgust toward management and not in the mood to discuss it.

Instead of going to the job site the next morning, I went to the office, where I asked the engineer to talk to the owner about reviewing Rocco's situation with his foreman. He told me he was sorry, but there was nothing he could do.

"If Rocco is not welcome here anymore," I said, "there is no way I can stay."

"We don't want you to quit," he said. "We're very happy with your performance. What if we entice you with a nice increase in your pay check?" he asked with a guilty smile.

"It's not about money; it's about friendship," I said. "If you can't help my friend stay on, I have no option but to move on as well."

Chapter 27

I could see from his expression that he was sorry he couldn't help me. "I wish I could change your mind and convince you to stay. You could have a good future here with us."

"It's been a pleasure working with you, and I thank you very much for the opportunity you gave me, and for all your help and your trust in me." Then I shook his hand and left.

In that specific moment, without realizing it, I was closing one chapter in my life and opening another.

I went directly to Rocco's home after I left the office, rang the doorbell, and waited. When he opened the door, he was very surprised to see me. I told him I had quit my job.

He said I shouldn't have done that—I had a family to consider.

I looked him straight in the eyes. "Get some decent clothes on," I said. "You and I are looking for a new job."

He hugged me and thanked me for my friendship.

After a few days of looking for work in vain, Rocco suggested that if we went to a larger company, we would find work immediately. I reminded him how I felt about that, and we continued our search.

One evening we heard on the news that the Construction Union had reached no agreement on its new contract with the committee representing the Building Contractors' Coalition. That meant the construction industries were going on strike, and the strike would last until an agreement was reached. In the meantime, of course, we had zero hope of finding work in the construction industry.

Rocco suggested it might be wise to take advantage of the strike and get our company started at once. Then, at the end of the strike, instead of looking for employment, we could begin working on our own.

"The working season is almost over," I said, "and since we have no idea when the strike will end or how tough it will be to get through it, I think it makes more sense to wait till next year, just as we planned."

"I'm tired of looking for work with these Mickey Mouse Italian-owned construction companies. It's humiliating to be rejected by our countrymen over and over again."

Over the duration of the strike, Pina and I had to spend our savings in order to pay our bills. Most of that money had been earmarked for a car, and the remainder for start-up costs of the new company. After having depleted our savings in full, we dug into the money we had been saving to pay the home mortgage, which was due at the end of the year.

Naturally, I found the situation extremely distressing. Everything I had planned with so much faith and hope was vanishing before my eyes. Due to lack of funds, come spring, I would not be able to start my business.

I tried to react in a positive way, but the more I attempted to remove negative ideas from my mind, the more I realized the stupidity of thinking money would be available when I needed it. I was simply deluding myself to consider such a scenario.

As I revisited my worst-case scenario, I received a phone call from Rocco saying he wanted to speak with me. He arrived half an hour later and we went out for a walk.

"I'm convinced this is the right time to get started with our company," he said. "As soon as the strike is over, we'll be ready to go."

I told him such a move was impossible at the moment—maybe even forever.

He asked me why I was so pessimistic.

Clenching my teeth to avoid crying, I replied, "I used up all my savings during the strike, as well as the money I collected from rentals to pay the mortgage. It's not only a question of being broke, but probably of losing the houses as well."

He shook his head, looking almost amused. "You worry too much. A bank loan would solve everything."

"There's no way I can get a bank loan without a job," I said. "With all the banks in Montreal, surely there's one among them that will take the chance on you. And that's all it takes—just one." He patted me on the shoulder. "See you later, friend."

I reflected on Rocco's advice. The more I thought about it, the

Chapter 27

more I was convinced he was right—perhaps there was no justification for feeling so desperate. Pina also agreed. I was the only one holding back.

In bed that night, I asked myself if I should follow Rocco's advice or wait. When I thought about going ahead with our plans, I felt a great sense of relief and security—indicating, I presumed, that I was on the right track. When I asked if I should wait, I felt fear and insecurity, which, I presumed, signified the wrong path.

Then I asked myself if I was able to get a loan. In asking that question, I felt a sense of peace.

After arriving at that perception, I was finally able to sleep.

As soon as I woke up the next morning, I noticed that I was more relaxed and calm, as though I had won a fearsome battle. I told Pina the nature of my perceptions.

She said my perceptions were always a good omen, and we should follow the new path they revealed. Hesitantly, I asked about her true opinion of me—if she thought I had the ability, the strength, and the willpower to successfully tackle the difficulties we would encounter once we started the business. And what would be her reaction if things took a turn for the worst.

With an expression of infinite love, she assured me she had no doubts about my capabilities—if I were to undertake my duties with diligence and, above all, without falling prey to fear, there was nothing to hold me back from achieving my goals.

"You know my loving you was never conditional on your financial success," she said. "I have always loved you for the man you are and not for what you could give me in the form of financial or material things. The one thing I want from you more than anything in the world is that you love me and the children, all the time."

I hugged her and, looking at the sky through the window, I said, "With God's help and yours, sooner or later we will be blessed by success. Now is probably the best time to lay the foundation for rebuilding our lives."

Later that day, I went to see Rocco to let him know I was ready to start our business, reminding him that Gioacchino would be a partner. He was very receptive and proposed we drink a toast to the success of our enterprise.

I promised myself that from that moment on I would practice everything I had learned on the power of thought. I would also spend some time in daily prayer to God, who remained a great mystery to me, as I did not know how He functioned or how He influenced the course of our lives.

Accordingly, I wrote the following prayer:

My God, I beseech You to help me overcome all the obstacles I meet at work and in my daily life. I beg You to guide, inspire, and protect me in all my endeavors. I also pray You to strengthen my character and willpower so that I may be brave and determined, capable of making the right decisions. I fervently call upon You to inspire and guide me to the bank that will lend me the necessary money to establish our enterprise. I beg You to crown my wishes with success.

I repeated this prayer many times a day and then at night in bed, until I fell asleep.

One day I bumped into Ruben, a man who worked for the contractor I had rented the apartment from when I came from Winnipeg. He greeted me cordially and asked what I was doing. I explained I was currently unemployed because of the strike, but that at the same time, I was getting ready to start a small asphalt-paving company. He said there was a lot of competition in that type of work, and that it might not be expedient for me to start out in that field. "If I were you, I would consider doing form work for concrete structure of houses and commercial foundations. There's a lot more opportunity there, less competition, and you can work pretty much straight through the year."

"I've never done that type of work."

"If you want to go into the form work business, you don't need to be an expert. You just hire a foreman who knows his craft and he takes over from there. All you need to do is find clients and manage the company." He said he was confident I had the ability to run a company, and didn't understand why I hesitated. "Let me know if you decide to follow my advice, and I'll talk to the owner of my company and get you a contract for building basements—on condition, of course, that your prices are competitive."

I thanked him for his advice and then we departed.

While driving I analyzed Ruben's suggestion. On one hand, the idea of working in a field with less competition and the possibility of year-round work were appealing. On the other hand, the fact that I had no experience and I had to rely entirely on the judgment and the ability of someone else made me very nervous, bringing to mind the reasons for the financial disaster of Winnipeg. I felt confused and filled with fear.

When I got home, I told Pina about my meeting with Ruben, and that I was feeling confusion and fear. After thinking for a while, she admitted she shared my concerns, and suggested I discuss the matter with Rocco.

Rocco thought it was a terrific idea—particularly because we could work straight through the winter months. I brought to his attention that I had no experience in the field, but that did not concern him at all, as he had worked for a form company for two years prior to meeting with me and felt completely comfortable in the business. He also said he knew plenty of people who did that kind of work, and we would not have any trouble getting good help. "We're lucky you met up with Ruben when you did. His idea makes total sense for us."

I repeated my concerns about my lack of experience, but he stopped me with a wave of his hand. "You have to trust me on this, Paolo. It's perfect for us. You've got to stop worrying."

After a long debate and still filled with fears and doubts, I caved in to Rocco's wishes and agreed to follow his advice. "Tomorrow, first thing, I will apply for the bank loan. This way, as soon as the strike ends, we'll be ready to get to work."

That evening, in the peace and silence of the night after Pina put the children to bed, I fervently prayed to God for help in getting the loan.

The following day I talked to the bank manager, who turned me down flat because I was not working. I left feeling dejected. Then I went to another bank, and another, and still another. I received the same rejection everywhere I went, and for the same reason—I was not working.

One day around ten o'clock in the morning, I decided to go to a nearby Italian coffee shop, promising Pina I would be back around noon. As I was driving, I passed a small bank where we had an account and where from time to time I went to cash my pay check.

The moment I saw the bank sign, I felt compelled to see the manager for the loan, despite the fact I barely knew him. I followed my instinct and parked the old truck about a block away from the bank, fearing that if the manager saw me driving that old vehicle, it would diminish my credibility and would influence his decision negatively. I went straight to his office, keeping a good thought, and asked his secretary if I might see him. She told me he was busy but should be free before long, if I cared to wait. I waited about fifteen minutes, and when I was finally summoned to his desk, he recognized me immediately and motioned for me to sit down. "What can I do for you today, Mr. Ficara?"

After gathering my self-confidence, I told him I needed a loan. He listened intently and said, "Would you mind answering a few of the usual questions—like where you work, your income, your rent, that sort of thing?" There it was again, I told myself.

I told him that because of the strike I was not working at the moment, but that I owned two buildings—one with three units and one with six. My family and I resided in one of the apartments in the six-unit dwelling. I explained how much I paid for them, the amount I collected in rentals, and the payments I made on the mortgage.

"Technically," he said, "I shouldn't be able to give you a loan because you are unemployed. But since you and your wife own two pieces of real estate, you seem stable enough to warrant the loan. Let me see if I can help you out." With a smile on his lips, he asked how much money I needed.

Relaxing now, I said jokingly, "I'll take whatever you can give me."

He laughed and said, "I can give you $5,000.00, since that is the maximum you can get without having to apply to the main office."

Since I felt certain my application would be rejected considering my lack of employment, I happily accepted the $5,000.00 loan. The secretary drew up the papers, which we signed on the spot. "Would you like a bank draft, or do you want to deposit this in your savings account?" he asked.

I took the latter, and shook his hand. Embarrassed by my emotions, I spoke in a barely audible voice, "Thank you for putting your trust in me. I will never forget this moment."

I left the bank elated, and couldn't wait to share the news with Pina.

Later that day, Rocco and I went to see a lawyer to draw up the papers for establishing our company. Gioacchino was to be an equal shareholder with Rocco and me. Afterward, I went to see Ruben to tell him the news of our new company—and that as soon as the strike was over we would begin our operation. He handed me some work plans for an upcoming job, assuring me that as long as our bid was competitive, he would give us the contract.

I went straight to see Rocco with a projection for our daily output. Based on that projection, we prepared a bid, which was accepted by Rubin immediately.

A few days later, I attended a party where I saw Pina's cousins—the Salvo brothers and their brother-in-law, *Zio (uncle) Nino*. They asked what and how I was doing. I told them we were doing well and that we were in the process of starting the form work company. *Zio (uncle) Nino* informed me that very soon they would be starting construction of their new company headquarters, and they needed someone to construct the concrete foundation walls. Would I give them a bid?

I consulted with Rocco and gave them a bid, which they accepted on the spot. In a way I was very happy we had begun to secure some work. But I couldn't help but wonder why both these companies had accepted my price so easily.

It was already October. We heard the Construction Workers' Union and the Contractors' and Developers' Committee were ready to reach an agreement. It wouldn't be long before we would be getting back to work—this time for ourselves.

I told Rocco it was time to find a good supervisor and a carpenter, since it would be more difficult to find good help once the strike was over. Rocco said he was going to see a Frenchman named Roger, who had once been his foreman, and an Italian named Pasquale, a carpenter with whom he once worked.

Not long thereafter, Rocco and I met with Roger and Pasquale individually, and they both told us exactly the same thing—they would be happy to work with us, but considering we were a new company we might not be able to offer them the stability of long-term work. They quickly reconsidered when I promised them a dollar an hour more than the Union and a guarantee of at least forty hours a week. They accepted my proposal without question. Now I had to find a commercial bank where we could open an account.

I called a man named Franco who owned a small asphalt company where I had worked earlier in the year. We had become good friends and I felt comfortable asking his advice. He volunteered to call his bank manager and introduce Rocco and me.

On the way to the bank, I explained to Franco that besides a checking account, we needed a credit line of approximately $10,000.00 because the $7,500.00 that we had on hand—representing contributions from

Rocco, Gioacchino and me—was earmarked for supplies. The credit would allow us to meet our daily expenses and weekly payroll while we waited to collect payment on our jobs.

Franco was pessimistic. He reminded us that we were a new and unproven company with no track record. A few years earlier, when he started his company, he had to wait six months before being considered for a small line of credit. Of course, now he could get all the credit he needed.

"We won't be able to begin operations without credit," I said.

"It wouldn't hurt to ask," Franco replied, "but don't be disappointed if you get turned down. It's the way banks operate. They want to make sure you are able to run a company before they see you as a good risk."

I understood what he was saying, even though it wasn't what I wanted to hear. When we arrived at the bank, Franco introduced us to the manager, saying he had known us for a long time and we were good and honest people with a deep sense of responsibility. After listening to Franco, the manager asked us what we had in mind.

I said we were about to start a company of form work to construct foundation for residential homes and commercial buildings, and wanted to open a checking account with his bank, where we would deposit the sum of $7,500.00. I asked if he would be willing to grant us a credit line of $10,000.00. He asked us how much experience we had. Rocco told him he had two years of experience, while I had to admit I had no experience at all.

The manager shook his head and said the bank's regulations clearly stipulated they could not accommodate any sort of loan to people without a provable track record of work skills and management. He thanked me for my honesty and added that if we opened a checking account with his bank, he would be able to reconsider his position in six months, based upon our performance in the interim.

"I don't see why we should open an account with your bank if there's no trust on your part," I said.

"This is not a matter of trust, and I certainly don't mean to offend you. These rules are based upon past experience on the part of lending organizations. If you as an individual were working, I could give you a $10,000.00 loan right now, but as a business entity I can't do that until you can prove you are capable of successfully managing the company. If I were to give you a loan, and you subsequently got into trouble, I could lose my job."

As he spoke, I thought about the Winnipeg misadventure, and was completely able to relate to his reasoning. But because we needed his help, I had to press him further, so I looked him in the eyes and said, "While everything you are saying may be true, you can't always go by the book alone to make an intelligent decision. There are more important considerations, such as character and reputation."

I had his attention, so I continued, "If the bank is not willing to take a risk with us, I don't see any reason to open an account here. If, on the other hand, the bank were willing to take a chance with us, we would never forget the favor, and you would have our company's account as long as we're in business."

After reflecting a moment, the manager smiled at me. "In all the years I've been a banker, no one has ever talked to me the way you have." He paused, turned his head down, took a deep breath, and said, "For once, I'm going to break the rules. I'll grant you a credit line of $3,500.00 to get you started—on one condition. That you pay very close attention to what you are doing and promise me if you find yourself in any sort of difficulty, you will come to me immediately."

"We will never put you in jeopardy with your superiors or make you sorry you took a chance with us," I said.

He smiled and said that he hoped his cooperation would contribute to the achievement of our goals and this would be the first step in a long and mutually prosperous relationship. Then, he turned to his secretary, instructing her to prepare all the necessary paperwork.

Once we were out of the bank, Rocco and Franco congratulated me. They were both surprised by the way things had worked out—

how the manager had reacted to my words, and the concessions he made in our favor. I said that I too was happy and astonished since I spoke only from instinct, unconcerned with the reaction I might get from the manager.

The next day, Rocco and I went to buy a beautiful, brand-new GMC 3/4-ton, four-wheel drive pickup truck. Four days later, the strike ended. Full of enthusiasm and hope, we started our first job—building an 825 foot-long, six-foot high concrete wall for Pina's cousins, the Salvo family.

I found it difficult to believe our fortune: what a few weeks before had seemed just an impossible dream had become an incredible reality.

Paolo's journey continues
with

Volume II
Healing Experiences

and

Volume III
Questions Answered
and
Goals Achieved

If you have any questions or comments for the
author, please contact him by using
the form on the website:
www.journeyofahealer.com

Made in the USA
Middletown, DE
22 June 2015